D0817666

...re my heart with you

My eyes will reflect your smile when you see me

At your side.
Now is what will matter to both of us.

Old is my body, but it is not who I am.
Loving me, you will know that I am wise,
Devoted and worthy of being valued.

Days together will become
Our happy adventure.
Go. Find me. I'm waiting for you.

Old Dog Haven

Every Old Dog Has a Story to Tell

Miranda

Ardeth De Vries

Bennett & Hastings Publishing
Seattle

Copyright © 2014 Ardeth DeVries

All rights reserved. No part of this book may be reproduced or transmitted in any form by any means, electronic or mechanical, including photocopying and recording, or by any information storage and retrieval system, except as may be expressly permitted by the 1976 Copyright Act or the publisher. Requests for permission should be made in writing to: Bennett & Hastings Publishing, c/o the address posted at www.bennetthastings.com.

Because of the dynamic nature of the Internet, any web addresses or links contained in this book may have changed since publication and no longer be valid.

The views expressed in this work are solely those of the author and do not necessarily reflect the views of the publisher, and the publisher hereby disclaims any responsibility for them.

Unless otherwise credited, photographs are from the personal collection of the author.

Bennett & Hastings titles may be ordered through booksellers or by writing the publisher at either sales@bennetthastings.com or 2400 NW 80th Street #254, Seattle WA 98117.

Celeste Bennett & George Hastings make their contribution to this work in memory of Molly.

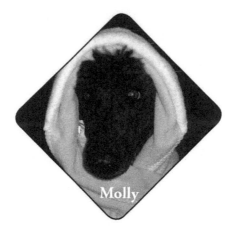

Molly

Front and back cover photographs by Julie Austin (www.anypetphotography.com). Front cover: former Old Dog Haven Ambassador Solomon. Back cover: Theodora (top left) and Lucky.
Photo of Molly, above, courtesy of the Harris family.
Front cover design by Steve Ford
Back cover design by Joe Myers

Library of Congress Control Number: 2014941776

Contents

Pat Colyar and Berta

Roland Lesta and Edgar

THIS BOOK IS DEDICATED TO ALL OLD DOGS, WITH THE HOPE THAT YOU HAVE PEOPLE WHO LOVE YOU AND VALUE YOUR PRESENCE IN THEIR LIVES

Melanie Granfors and Maxwell

Joe Myers and Snooki

Duke

ACKNOWLEDGMENTS

Many thanks to the following people who not only provided information and stories about the dogs featured in this book, as well as photographs, but who welcomed them into their homes and hearts and allowed their voices to be heard:

Barb Bauer, Darci Bonsen, Marty Crowley, Julie Cunningham, Amy Devon, Cheryl Fontaine, Janine Henkel, Kathy Jackson, Paula Jennings, Ron Kerrigan, Noel Kjosness, Janice Kugler, Linda, Trisha Lovgren, Kelly Marlo, Priscilla McCarty, Robyn Miller, Tina Nabseth, Katie Parries, Judith and Lee Piper, Judy Pulley, Rhonda Rowe, Yvonne Sauter, Jan Schwenger, Mary Staberg, Erica Stewart, and Valerie Watson.

Thank you to the following people who also provided photographs:

Karen Ducey (Sparkle and Tanner), Kim (Baloo), Dana (Baloo and Mollee), Dr. Jared O'Connor (Gretchen and Barb and Bob Bauer), Mary Jo Adams (Duke: Acknowledgments), Lisa Black (Bubbles: Introduction), Michelle Krivacek (Miranda: Title Page), Donna Gonder (Sparky: End-Of-Life Decisions), Jim Ito (Melanie Granfors: Dedication Page), and Paula Moreschi (Joe Myers: Dedication Page).

A very special thanks to Old Dog Haven's "honorary" photographer, Julie Austin, (voted Best Pet Photography in Evening Magazine's 2012 & 2013 The Best of Western Washington) for the front cover photograph of Solomon, the back cover photographs of Theodora and Lucky, the first photograph of Ozzie in his chapter, Roger (Plan Ahead), Noses (Supplementary Material), Pat (Dedication Page), Roland (Dedication Page) Felix (Chapter Three), Matthew (When An Animal Friend Dies), and me (About the Author). More of Julie Austin's work can be viewed at www.anypetphotography.com

Thank you to my design guru Joe Myers for his technical assistance and valuable input for the back cover.

Thank you to Steve Ford for enhancing, converting and using his magic touch on <u>all</u> of the photographs in the book. (PhotosbySteveFord.com) (WebsitesBySteveFord.com)

To my readers, Judith Piper and Marcy Bahr: thank you for your time, input, and support.

To <u>everyone</u> in the Old Dog Haven family: thank you for your dedication and commitment to senior dogs.

Thank you to *New York Times* bestselling author, Louise Penny, who graciously gave permission to use a quote from her book, *A Fatal Grace,* in the chapter about Baloo.

Thank you to my publisher, Celeste Bennett, Co-Founder of Bennett & Hastings, Publishers, LLC, for your commitment to this project, your generosity of spirit, your attention to detail, your wit and humor, and for making it possible for my vision of this book to find its way to the printed (and online) page. It's a pleasure to work with you.

A very special thank you to Solomon, whose beautiful face graces the cover of this book. Sol was taken in by Old Dog Haven in 2009 at age twelve and he lived for five wonderful years with Final Refuge mom Lisa Black before he left his body in February of this year. Sol was a wonderful ambassador for Old Dog Haven. We remember him with love and are thankful for his presence in our lives.

Thank you to all of the dogs featured in this book for the many lessons you teach by example.

Something WAY BEYOND thank you to Judith and Lee Piper for their willingness to make such a HUGE difference in the lives of homeless senior dogs. You are truly the heart of Old Dog Haven.

Paws up to all of you!

OLD DOG HAVEN FOUNDERS: JUDITH AND LEE PIPER

"Somebody needs to do this … "

Judith and Bodie   *Lee and Victor*

How does it happen that an equestrian specialist/business woman and a chemical engineer create an organization like Old Dog Haven? It's really a matter of readiness, timing and, in this case, a series of phone calls. All of these factors resulted in a few old dogs finding a home with Judith and Lee Piper in late 2004. Of course it was also helpful that both of these amazing people had signs tattooed on their foreheads that said, "Old Dogs Welcome."

In an interview with the *Seattle Times* Judith was asked how it all began and she said, "I started dog-walking at a shelter and met a woman through horses who did dog rescue. My husband and I took in two dogs at the very end of their lives through this woman. We got a great deal of satisfaction from it and decided that it was needed and that we could do it and therefore we should. Lee and I both felt that somebody needs to do this. Dogs just can't be abandoned at the very end of their lives. We had NO clue where this would lead us!"

How often have you heard someone say, "Somebody needs to do something"? What usually happens is that there's a great wringing of hands, but nothing much actually happens. It's often easier to just sit back and wait for someone else to do what needs to be done. People don't always walk their talk. But Judith and Lee did. They still do.

Initially, the idea was to provide hospice care and to take in one dog at a time, but somehow—as is often true with rescue work—the word got out. Very quickly, Judith and Lee were receiving requests from shelters and rescue groups to take in their older dogs. Eventually, staff and volunteers who were affiliated with local shelters, as well as independent rescue groups, began sending in donations in addition to requests for help. The generosity of others was very welcome since the Pipers were using their personal financial resources to care for the dogs they rescued and the need was far greater than funds available.

In the early days of 2005 the Old Dog Haven website (www.olddoghaven. org) was created by Ron Kerrigan. Judith and Lee met Ron when they adopted their beloved Gabriel from the Whidbey Island Animals' Improvement shelter on Whidbey Island, and he offered his computer expertise to develop and maintain a website for Old Dog Haven. Ron no longer maintains the website, but his contribution to Old Dog Haven with the original website and in many other areas is very much appreciated.

"By then," Judith says, "we knew that we were really serious about this work."

In the late months of 2004, Old Dog Haven officially became a tax-exempt nonprofit organization.

As news about Old Dog Haven continued to spread among the shelter community, it became clear that Judith and Lee couldn't possibly keep all the old dogs that needed homes at their own house, so they began to search for other people who were willing to care for older dogs. The "if you build it they will come" principle worked beautifully as people began to volunteer to take in the dogs that needed homes.

Even though the Pipers originally had no intention of doing adoption work, they found that some old dogs abandoned in shelters were very adoptable. As a result, a network of foster homes was created to care for adoptable dogs until they found their own forever homes.

For the dogs that were not healthy enough or emotionally fit for adoption, the concept of Final Refuge homes was born. Final Refuge homes offer hospice care for dogs that need one last secure home, with all medical costs covered by Old Dog Haven, for the remainder of the dogs' lives.

The number of active foster and Final Refuge homes has increased from just one in 2005 to over 135 as of the date of this writing. But there still aren't enough homes to accommodate the long list of older dogs that are dying by inches in shelters.

Home Base or foster dogs to the vet. The days are long, dinner doesn't usually happen until around 9:30 P.M., and nights are often interrupted by dogs that need attention. This labor of love by two people who care enough to devote their lives to old dogs speaks for itself in so many ways.

The essence of who Judith and Lee are—as human beings and animal stewards—is defined by this work. Their lives have gone to the dogs, and they wouldn't have it any other way.

OLD DOG HAVEN: WHAT WE DO AND HOW WE DO IT

*We think of ourselves as a family, and anyone who becomes
involved with our work becomes part of our family.*

You've probably figured this out after reading the previous chapter, but just to be clear: Old Dog Haven is not a shelter. All of our senior dogs (eight years or older) live happily in homes with foster and Final Refuge families who love and cherish them as valued family members. Old Dog Haven only takes in dogs from western Washington.

We provide temporary foster care for dogs that are adoptable and have a reasonable life expectancy. Foster dogs typically stay with their foster parents anywhere from a few weeks to several months, depending on how long it takes to place the dogs into their permanent homes. Since 2005 through the end of 2013, 1,441 Old Dog Haven dogs have been adopted.

We provide permanent Final Refuge care for dogs that are too old for adoption, perhaps in the last months or year of their lives or in fragile health. Our goal is that their last months or years be happy and that they die safe and at peace, knowing they are loved. As time has passed, we have increasingly taken in more and more dogs that are not adoptable and have ended up in shelters at the very end of their lives. In these cases, all we can do is bring them to a safe loving place for a day or a few days of hospice care before they experience a gentle peaceful death with someone who will grieve for them.

All veterinary care and medical expenses for foster and Final Refuge dogs are paid for by Old Dog Haven.

We also assist individuals, shelters and other rescue groups in their efforts to find homes for their senior dogs.

We do this work because too many dogs of advanced years find themselves terrified and confused at shelters, where their chances of being adopted are almost zero. According to a 2012 study by the American Humane Society 60% of the dogs in shelters are euthanized. A dog is killed in a shelter in the U.S. approximately every nine seconds, and the first casualties are always senior dogs because people don't go to a shelter to adopt an older dog. In fact, the AHS states that only 20% of all dogs in shelters are adopted, and those dogs are generally less than two years old. Other senior dogs are desperate for homes, often because life-changing circumstances have altered their family dynamics and their people are either no longer willing or no longer able to provide them a home.

We rely on our foster and Final Refuge parents as well as our generous donors to keep the dogs in our care comfortable and happy during their time with us. Our veterinary expenses are very high (approximately $40,000 per month in 2013) as we try to bring our dogs back to the best possible health. Most dogs come to us in poor physical condition, and helping them is sometimes challenging and often expensive. Yet, many return to healthy, happy lives after receiving good care and medical treatment. Others spend a shorter time with us and die peacefully, surrounded by love.

Old Dog Haven is an IRS-approved 501(c)(3) nonprofit charitable organization. We rely on donations for our income. We do not receive any government funds.

But there's more. Just saying that Old Dog Haven takes in senior dogs doesn't even come close to explaining how the organization actually works and what it takes to keep things going.

There's transportation to consider. The logistics of getting dogs from shelters to foster/Final Refuge homes often creates a complicated puzzle that can only be solved by many people working together. Dozens of dogs need to be transported every year. Our Placement/Transport Coordinator, Tina Nabseth, does it all with a smile because she has many people on whom she can depend for this important task. Sometimes, if long distances need to be covered, we use a relay system of volunteers who meet each other at various points along a particular route. (A transport volunteer once asked Judith if pot-lucks could be arranged at the rest stops along I-5.) When our transport volunteers get "the

call" from Tina, they somehow manage to adjust their schedules and get the job done. (We have one transport volunteer who drove 500 miles in one day just to get a dog to his new home.) For the dogs that meet our dedicated drivers the world instantly becomes a better place. They're being chauffeured by someone who cares about them and wishes them well on the first lap of their journey to a new life.

Then there are the veterinarians who take such good care of our dogs. Some dogs are in very bad shape when they leave a shelter, and they need to be taken to the vet immediately. Our vets always make time for critical

Transport volunteer, Kathryn Harnecker and Mr. Muffet on their way to his forever home on Vancouver Island.

cases and are willing to see dogs with urgent medical needs right away. Because our foster and Final Refuge homes are located all over western Washington many different veterinarians provide whatever medical care is needed. Our "home clinic," Frontier Village Veterinary Clinic, has seen more than 900 Old Dog Haven dogs. It's not unusual for us to have as many as four dogs there on any given day.

When dogs are taken in by Old Dog Haven, at the very minimum they receive a complete vet exam, which includes vaccinations, a blood panel, and—on an as needed basis— X-rays and dental procedures (often very extensive). If further care is in-

Dr. Jared O'Connor visits with Final Refuge dog, Lyle.

dicated, surgery is required, or a chronic condition needs consistent treatment, these problems are taken care of for as long as the dog is with us. Sometimes the vet care is quite expensive, and we're able to do this thanks to the generosity of our donors. We even have a special fund called The Maranda Fund, established to set aside funds for unusually expensive procedures.

Every day we're constantly reminded of the kindness and generosity of people as they donate money, supplies and time, organize fundraisers, host benefits, offer discounted services, and in general, take the initiative to help us care for our dogs:

- a local car dealership donated a van,
- our dogs have received free water therapy,
- Scott Watkins, a real estate agent with an artistic eye, has turned his vehicle into a mobile billboard for Old Dog Haven,
- a mobile groomer visits foster homes,
- printers offer discounted services,
- artists and writers donate proceeds from their work, and
- professional photographers volunteer to photograph our dogs.
- In 2010, a dedicated team of volunteers orchestrated the first Old Dog Haven auction, which generated thousands of dollars to be used to help old dogs.

Mark Malnes, owner of Savage Color in Seattle, offers discounted printing services to Old Dog Haven. Mark is pictured here with adopted Old Dog Haven dog, Thunder.

In July 2013, Old Dog Haven Board members Lisa Black and Paula Moreschi organized the second annual "Walk For Old Dogs and Old Dog Olympiad," which was truly an amazing event. Three hundred people and their senior dogs gathered at the Bellevue Town Park to celebrate at what certainly must have been the largest gathering of old dogs ever held in the United States. Senior dogs of all breeds, shapes and sizes, dogs with only three legs, dogs with two legs wheeling themselves in carts, and dogs riding in strollers all strutted their stuff in the opening promenade as an Olympic torch was passed down the line of participants. Medals were awarded in various events, dogs happily socialized with each other while their human companions bragged about them, and the positive energy in the park was palpable. I had tears in my eyes as I watched this incredible display of love for old dogs by people who were so proud of their senior canine companions.

You can even "like" us on Facebook, and you can buy Old Dog Haven merchandise at various businesses, thanks to volunteers who have developed these opportunities for people to learn about and support Old Dog Haven. You can also apply for and use the Old Dog Haven VISA card. Old Dog Haven receives money for each new card when it is first used, and a percentage of every dollar charged to the card thereafter.

Generosity isn't limited to adults either: Girl Scouts, like Troop 52539, make dog bed covers, young children decide that helping old dogs is more important than receiving gifts so they ask for donations to Old Dog Haven instead of birthday presents, school classes sponsor dogs, and young adults organize dog walks and neighborhood benefits for Old Dog Haven. These

Crowd favorite, Captain Wrinkles, won a gold medal in the 50-yard Crawl, proving that slow and steady does win the race.

Girl Scout Troop 52539

self-generated donation activities provide a solid foundation for the haven we create for old dogs. We couldn't possibly do what we do without the help of those who care as much as we do.

But there's more. Our donors, at the very least, deserve thanks for their efforts on behalf of our dogs, so that means thank-you notes. Even though we've grown over the years, the essence of what Old Dog Haven is all about is very personal, so all of our thank-you notes are hand written by dedicated volunteers who are very much appreciated for their efforts.

There are also events to attend. We're always trying to involve more people in our cause, so that means exposure. We try to attend as many events as we can during the year to spread the word about Old Dog Haven. The booth, supplies, and volunteers who give Old Dog Haven a presence at such events wouldn't be there without organization, and we're very thankful for the multi-tasking skills of Events Coordinator Gabrielle Flanagan. We're also fortunate to have volunteers who love to schmooze and are happy to attend various events, usually with dogs, to tell people about Old Dog Haven.

Telling people about our dogs and the people who contribute so much to Old Dog Haven also happens through our newsletters. We publish six newsletters a year: three are E-newsletters that can be viewed online, and three are print newsletters. Once again, these efforts require people, like our "Mailing Warriors" who take care of the labeling and distribution of print newsletters. We also have a brochure about Old Dog Haven that we hand out at various events.

Getting the word out in their own style of meeting and greeting, Genese Harney and Donna Adams set up a table in front of local grocery stores once a

The dog pictured with Genese (L) and Donna is former Final Refuge dog, Rosie, who loved to schmooze with people who stopped by to visit.

month, year 'round, just to spread the word about Old Dog Haven. These two intrepid supporters raise thousands of dollars each year through their efforts.

Even family members of Board members and volunteers step up to transport dogs, host benefits, and do whatever is needed to help our senior dogs.

In short, we couldn't possibly do what we do without the support of hundreds of people who give so generously of their time, energy and money.

Since Old Dog Haven was created in late 2004, the organization has grown beyond all expectations, but at the heart of what we do is the original mission: get old dogs out of shelters so they don't die alone and afraid. Doing this work is very personal for all of us involved in Old Dog Haven. We think of ourselves as a family, and anyone who becomes involved with our work becomes extended family. Yes, we look like an organization on the surface, but beneath the organizational façade is a family structure that speaks of family values, dedication and commitment.

Felix

HOW DOGS COME TO OLD DOG HAVEN

Their value in the eyes of others has diminished,
and they've become expendable.

Now you know a little about the people who started Old Dog Haven and have a basic understanding of the kind of care we offer old dogs, as well as a sense of appreciation for the many people involved in our work. Next, I'd like to help you understand how and why senior dogs come to us, before you meet the dogs featured in this book. The bottom line is the same for all of them: no one wants them. Their value in the eyes of others has diminished, and they've become expendable.

There are, however, specific circumstances that create situations in which old dogs are abandoned. In the following chapters, you'll read about thirty-four dogs that represent various circumstances in which old dogs become homeless. You'll also see how Old Dog Haven helped these dogs gain value in the eyes of others and become "no longer expendable."

- Many of our dogs were cherished companions of elderly people who died or had to move to an assisted living facility that won't allow dogs. The family either won't take the dog or there is no family to assume responsibility for the dog.

- Economic hardships cause a family to lose their home and the dog becomes homeless too.
- People divorce and neither person wants the dog.
- Children are born, and the dog isn't able to tolerate the young children, or the parents just don't want one more responsibility.
- Dogs are taken from hoarders.
- Dogs are removed from homes because of neglect.
- Puppy mills are raided by authorities and Old Dog Haven is asked to take the senior dogs.
- Dogs are abandoned in empty houses.
- Former show dogs are no longer useful and are brought to the vet to be euthanized.
- People move away and don't want to take the dog with them for various reasons.
- Dogs are brought to shelters as strays with no history at all. Many are in terrible shape, but some are relatively healthy. Many of these "strays" are found by the side of the road, often injured. Others are found wandering in neighborhoods. We suspect that a significant number of them are brought to shelters by their humans, who falsely claim that the dogs are strays so they don't have to pay a surrender fee.
- Lifetime human companions leave dogs at shelters.
- The dog has health issues the family doesn't want to deal with, either for financial reasons or because they just don't want to be bothered with a sick dog.
- Neighbors intervene on behalf of a neglected dog.
- People say they have no time for the dog.
- The dog is brought to the vet or to a shelter by the dog's human companion to be euthanized, but the vet or shelter feels that the dog has time left if given proper care and love.
- Another rescue group contacts Old Dog Haven because they have a senior dog that isn't adoptable and they would like Old Dog Haven to find a home for the dog.
- People call Old Dog Haven saying that they've rescued a dog and want us to take the dog, not understanding that we are only able to take dogs from an entity or individual who is in a position to transfer *legal* responsibility for them.

If you're horrified by some of the reasons given in the above list, you get to stand in line with the rest of us who care for old dogs. But here's the thing: We can't and don't focus on the actions of people who abandon old dogs. To spend energy being angry contaminates the positive energy we need to expend on our dogs. The dogs are the focus of our attention. I'm not saying we don't feel anger. Sometimes, we're absolutely appalled by the condition of some of our dogs when they come to us; how could anyone not be upset about an old dog left tied to a tree in front of an empty house? But we quickly move on to determine what we can do to help the dogs.

Choosing the dogs to feature in this book wasn't easy. All of our dogs and the people who saved them have stories to tell, but for this book the Pipers and I have chosen dogs that are representative of the scenarios I've just described.

Please join me in celebrating the transformation that occurred in the thirty-four dogs you'll read about in the following chapters.

BALOO

Much More Than Just a Hound Dog

This is a story about a dog that was classified as a "stray" by a large shelter that was his home for three weeks. The shelter never received a frantic call from people who found their much-loved dog missing and were hoping he'd been found and taken to the shelter. No one claiming to be his "owner" showed up asking to have the dog returned to him, as if he were some kind of possession that had been misplaced. (Just for the record, my use of the word "owner" in the previous sentence will be the first and last time you see it used by me in this book unless I'm quoting someone else.) I know that dogs are considered possessions in the eyes of the law, but in my world people who think they need to own a dog would really be better off buying a stuffed animal. Dogs are not possessions and deserve to be treated with love, dignity and respect.

The term "stray" as it is used by shelters is very misleading because the word suggests that homeless dogs just wander around and end up being found by people who bring them to shelters. These "stray" dogs don't just fall from the sky. They come from somewhere, and yet in so many cases, no one ever calls the shelter to ask if their missing dog is there.

Many people don't look for their dogs if they go missing. Some people even dump their dogs in neighborhoods or secluded areas because they don't want them any longer, and they don't care what happens to them. Or, in some stretch of logic they feel the dogs will be better off left to fend for themselves rather than being taken to a shelter.

Here's what happens to stray dogs:

- If no one finds the dog, he or she dies of starvation or exposure.
- Sometimes when someone finds a dog wandering, the "finder" attempts to find the dog's people and this conscientious behavior on the part of the rescuer often results in a happy reunion between the lost dog and the dog's family.
- If the dog was dumped and the dog's people aren't interested in claiming the dog, the rescuer keeps the dog, or perhaps attempts to find a home for the dog, or brings the dog to a shelter.
- Many dogs found wandering are picked up by Animal Control and brought to shelters.

Whether a stray dog is brought to a shelter by someone who found the dog, or a dog is brought to a shelter by Animal Control and no one ever calls the shelter about the dog, the bottom line is the same in both cases: no one wants the dog. Homeless dogs end up in shelters by the hundreds of thousands every day in the U.S. In most cases, no one calls about them and the dogs live in cages until they are either adopted or euthanized.

Old dogs are rarely adopted from shelters, so the old guys that are brought to shelters as "strays" and are never reunited with their people find themselves dying by inches in cages because no one wants them. Eventually they are euthanized.

But not Baloo.

Baloo charmed everyone he met at the shelter from the moment he arrived, so when no one ever called about him and no one was interested in adopting him, shelter staff called Old Dog Haven to see if we could place him in one of our Final Refuge homes. Yes, he was old. Yes, his appearance indicated that he'd been neglected for a long time. No, he didn't seem to be very healthy, but the shelter staff felt he deserved a second chance at happiness.

Right about the time the shelter contacted Judith about Baloo, Julie Cunningham appeared on the scene as someone interested in providing a foster home for an old dog. The short version of the story is that Julie bailed Baloo out of the slammer and ended up adopting him. Baloo lived happily with Julie and her family for about six months before his old body finally failed him. But, there's more to the story. Much more. Here's what Julie had to say when I asked her to tell me about Baloo:

"In May of 1999 I was going through an interesting time in my life. I had everything I thought I wanted: career (firefighter/EMT), boyfriend (not ready for marriage but still good), friends and good times. But I still felt lacking, and I wasn't sure what was missing. I finally decided, after much thought, that I'd like to get a dog. Not just any dog. I wanted a lab. I'd always wanted a dog of my own. My parents had brought a few dogs into our house and the dogs always 'left to go to a farm,' which was a not so nice way of saying, 'We gave them away.' I was crushed each time this happened.

"I'd met many dogs in my life and all of the labs I met seemed like they would be perfect dogs for me. I kept checking the paper for puppies (Give me a break. I know now that shelter dogs are better, but back then I was all about breeding and such) and found a good line on some excellent pups. I set off to Oregon to fetch my girl.

"She was ten weeks old and perfect. Fat tummy, needle teeth and oh so sweet puppy breath. I took thirty days off of work and trained her 24/7. I liked to refer to her as my 'first born.' Her name was Smokey. She was my best friend, my confidant, my everything. She lasted past the career, past the boyfriend, pretty much past everything.

"In November of 2009 I took Smokey in the middle of the night to be put down. I'd tried for days to follow the vet's recommendations to give her pain pills and IV fluids to no avail. It was her time. It was absolutely THE hardest thing I've ever had to do. The next day, I was such a wreck. My friends cared for me as if I had lost a child. I had. I didn't think I would ever recover.

"About a month later I began to notice my life was again lacking that certain something. I still missed Smokey fiercely, and I began to wonder if it could actually be true that I NEEDED a dog to be happy.

"So, I decided to try 'fostering' a dog. I knew I couldn't ever raise a puppy again. It's like raising a child. So many hours, such a short life-span. Not for me. I can't ever go through that again.

"I found a place called Old Dog Haven and learned that they only rescue older dogs. I decided that I wanted to 'temporarily' house a dog until she found her forever home. That way, I was just doing a favor, helping out an animal, and seeing her off to her new family. I would have the companionship without the heartache. No muss, no fuss. I contacted Judith (the Executive Director of Old Dog Haven) and told her I was only interested in female labrador retrievers. I still missed Smokey something fierce and was hoping to find a nice dog to foster that reminded me of her.

"Judith called me one day and told me there was a dog at the local humane society that was described by the shelter as a lab-mix. She told me I didn't have to feel obligated and just to check him out. I was skeptical because she mentioned 'him' and I knew I only wanted a female. My experience at that point was that female dogs were gentler than male dogs, not to mention they didn't go around humping everything.

"So off I went to the pound to check out a male dog I probably didn't want to foster. I was met by a volunteer who took me to the dog's kennel. The loud barking in the shelter really grated on my nerves, and I nearly walked out at that point. But, I stayed while the volunteer brought out a REALLY OLD dog, covered in matted hair. I took one look at the dog and decided he was NOT what I wanted. Even to foster. He was super old, REALLY smelly, and looked about three days from his last hurrah. 'Oh great,' I thought. I'd have to call Judith back and tell her I was shallow and mean and couldn't possibly foster him. I felt like a heel.

"The volunteer suggested we go outside and 'get to know each other.' Whatever. I'd already made up my mind about that particular hound. Oh, did I forget to mention that? Yes … he was a HOUND dog through and through. Perhaps basset/lab mix, but 'mix' was the closest he'd ever get to being called 'labrador' in his life. Still … the pound is a place that forces you to give chances where normally you'd just walk away.

"I went out to the painfully small exercise yard (probably a 6' by 20' gravel enclosure) and threw the ball for the poor creature. It was obvious within a few minutes he was totally deaf and nearly blind, but something about his eagerness to fetch the ball and bring it to me struck a chord. I decided I'd give him a month. He was friendly, a little shy, but eager to please. I knew I could at least give him a temporary home.

"So after a few minutes spent filling out paperwork, I loaded a horrible smelling dog into my car. My poor car. I don't think it has recovered yet. Poor guy was anxious about leaving the POUND. The place where old dogs like him get abandoned and put to sleep. He was whining and crying. I started to back out when a shelter worker ran out and banged on my window. 'I just wanted to see him one last time,' she said. Oh great. A hard case. He'd been there three weeks and had melted the hearts of everyone. Not me. I was just his temporary master.

"During the ride home he was still anxious, and when I brought him up my steps his effort was labor intensive. 'Oh great. An old, smelly, CRIPPLED dog,' I thought to myself.

"Once we got inside the house, something happened. He moved IMMEDIATELY to my side. Now, ordinarily, I wouldn't have thought anything but 'this poor dog is scared.' But he never left my side. If I went to the bathroom, there he was. If I got up to go to the kitchen, again, the dang dog pressed against my leg. After about 30 minutes of this, I started to warm up to him, so I took him outside and began the long, arduous task of grooming him.

"To say his grooming had been neglected is an understatement. The poor dog (I now imagine he has Husky mix as well) had at least three coats as far as I could see: a downy first layer, a long thin second layer, and a wiry third layer— none of which had been groomed for a VERY long time. I managed to get two large kitchen garbage bags full of dead hair from the poor guy. He looked like he'd lost 30 lbs when I was done.

"After the grooming, he continued to stick right by my side, pressing into me when I walked. My kids were due home on the school bus soon, so I needed to make sure he wasn't aggressive. I knelt down and softly tugged on his jowls as a child might. It was then I noticed he had no teeth. Well, he had stubs of teeth, but they were worn down to nubs. I knew I didn't have to worry about him mauling my children to death. Now I just had to wait and see if they would clobber *him*.

"On that front, my daughter Mollee, who is autistic, RAN up to him and began the longest petting session the poor fella had probably ever had. He's been 'her' dog ever since. He stands patiently while she adorns him with necklaces and hats all day long.

Baloo and Mollee

My son, who is severely autistic, does NOT like dogs. AT ALL. But he will run his fingers through this dog's coat.

"I named him Baloo, after the lovable, dopey, yet smart (in ways that count), bear from *The Jungle Book*.

"He's been a real blessing in our lives, and we ended up adopting him permanently. He's still kind of smelly and drools a lot. His breath smells like three day old dead fish left in the hot sun. But he still walks by my side from room to room. He's so trusting, sweet and good natured.

"I swear, Baloo is the BEST natural autism therapy dog! He just KNOWS when a child needs to have him near. My daughter's expressive language has exploded since we've had him, but it's not just Mollee who has been helped by Baloo. One day my friend's son Keneau, who is SEVERELY autistic, was outside with Baloo and all the other kids. I saw Keneau straddling Baloo. He had his arms wrapped around him and was just LOVING all over Baloo. Keneau was soooo CALM. He almost always is in constant rages, but not when he's with Baloo.

"It's incredible. I can't even put into words how most therapy dogs get at least a year of socialization and then specialized training, and Baloo manages to have it naturally. I'm so amazed by him I'm starting to wonder if he was guided to me.

Baloo and Keneau

"We'll be sad when it's his time to go. I went into this knowing he was older and wouldn't be around for too long, and so far he's doing great. He sleeps the sleep of a dog that can't remember ever having to be afraid or alone. In our bed. He does still occasionally wake up in the night to check to make sure I'm still there, which breaks my heart. Whatever he's gone through, he's got a good home now. We love him."

Julie wrote the above narrative about Baloo in 2010 when we featured him in one of our newsletters. During that same year he was also written about in *Dog Fancy* magazine.

Sadly, also in 2010, Julie had to say good-bye to her beloved Baloo. When I asked her to tell me about the experience of letting him go, here's what she had to say:

"I had a hard time taking him in to be put down because he was FINE two hours before.

"At least on his last day he got to go in the car to drop the kids off at school. He loved watching all the kids walk by the car. We also went to visit my mom and he liked to give big WOOFS to her little Yorkie.

"When we got up from our nap he couldn't walk and was clearly suffering from a left brain injury. I gave him about two minutes, praying maybe it was just his legs getting weak and then I KNEW it wasn't. I couldn't believe it. I was SURE he had a few more months at least.

"He normally LOVED going to the vet, but our vet was out to lunch so I had to go to animal emergency. Baloo had a very good sniffer and boy he did NOT like the smells at that place. I'm sure every animal that had marked their territory was under duress and he probably smelled that. After the exam and determination to put him down, I asked that the vet push the drugs outside. They inserted the catheter and I took him out.

"He was SO relieved but also much worse in the walking department. I held him up and we walked over to a nice shady tree. He lay down with me and I just stroked him for several minutes until he was relaxed. Then I called the office on my cell phone and told them to send the vet out. It was very peaceful as these things go, so I'm happy about that. One of the mistakes I made with Smokey was letting the vet tell me to wait a day to see if she got better. She suffered mightily and we ended up putting her down in the middle of the night. She couldn't even lift her head by the end, and I don't think she was aware of anything. I didn't want that to happen to Baloo.

"So, he was aware of me when he went and knew I had a hold of him and wouldn't let go. It wasn't easy, but it was definitely the right thing to do. I'm sad, but I know he had a great few months at his end.

"Mollee, on the other hand, is completely devastated. It's hard to explain to an autistic child about death—especially since Baloo was a happy doggy dropping her off at school just a few hours before. I'm working on looking for books that explain it better than I can."

So, that's Baloo's story. Baloo's life was transformed when he went from being an old, smelly, throw-away shelter dog to a much loved, productive member of a family. Julie's transformation began the moment she met Baloo and continued throughout the time he was with her. Mollee, Josef, Keneau and the other autistic children who spent time with Baloo were transformed because he gave them what they needed.

When Baloo finally left his body "his heart didn't so much stop as that he'd finally given it all away."[1]

---

[1] Louise Penny, *A Fatal Grace* (New York: Minotaur Books 2007)

LITTLE SIR GRUNTLY BEAR

*"I will never forget him and will always, always miss him
no matter how many dogs I love."*

Many of the older dogs that have come to Old Dog Haven over the years are what we call "elderly left-behinds." These dogs were beloved companions of older people who were no longer able to care for them because they had to leave their homes and become residents of nursing homes that don't allow dogs on the premises. This kind of separation is heart-breaking for both dog and human.

When Mark Engstrom died, his wife, Peggi, who suffered from numerous health issues, moved into a nursing facility. Their much loved dog, Little Sir Gruntly Bear, was brought to a boarding kennel. After seven long months in the kennel, Bear, age twelve and mostly blind, was taken into foster care by Old Dog Haven. While Bear was in the care of Old Dog Haven he received needed veterinary care and after a short time he was ready to be adopted.

Not many people are interested in adopting older dogs that don't see well, but when Judy Pulley saw the write-up about Bear on Old Dog Haven's website she says, "When I saw Bear's picture, something about him called to me." Judy was all too familiar with Bear's story because she and her husband had adopted another Lhasa, Toby, whose person had also gone into assisted living. Toby lived with the Pulley family for three years before they had to let him go, and they missed him so much they were ready to welcome another dog into their home and hearts.

Arrangements were made through Bear's foster family to transport him from his foster home in Mt. Vernon to Olympia. Judy says that Bear slept most of the way home, but "when we turned off onto our private road he got up and got on my lap to look out (at whatever he could see). When we stopped at our gate he started making his little grunty sounds. (Have you ever heard piglets grunt and squeal? That's what Bear sounded like.) He wanted out, so we left the truck outside the gate and walked in. Bear knew he was home."

Bear was introduced to Judy's other three dogs who acted "like nothing new was happening. One cat wasn't sure about the new guy, but the other two cats touched noses with Bear and went on their way."

One cat in particular, Georgette, adopted Bear as her own personal friend and became his seeing-eye cat. Georgette was born without a tail and is unable to walk properly (she hops like a rabbit) but Georgette took very good care of Little Bear. She would rub up against him when he was close to bumping into something, keeping him from falling down the only two stairs the Pulleys have in their home. On most nights Georgette could be found curled up next to Bear. She slept with him through the night. If he got up and moved, she did too.

Judy says, "Every day was brighter with Bear in my life. He was needy, but independent, stubborn, and eager to please. He was the boss and he had us all wrapped around his little paw. None of our dogs begged at the table until Bear came to live with us. By the time he started the barking at the table he was completely blind, but his sense of smell was super. Now, even though Bear is gone, his legacy of barking when he wanted something has been inherited by the other dogs. When our Molly starts barking for something I always think fondly of Little Sir Gruntly Bear.

"Bear loved to be with you, no matter where you were, whatever you were doing. Once when I was out of town my husband was working on the addition of a bedroom to our tiny little house. When I returned home I was told that Bear was right there with him all the time, helping him frame, install drywall, mud and paint. He was quite the little helper. I did notice some blue paint in his fur when I returned home—proof of his painting skills.

35

"Bear enjoyed his trips to 'Grandma' Betty's house (my mother-in-law who lives with us on our property.) He loved our grandkids and they were very respectful of him; they'd pat him on the head and call him 'Good Old Bear.' Bear stayed close while they played with their doll house. Given the chance, they would have liked to dress him up, but we suggested treats instead, and we knew that Bear was grateful."

As Bear aged his body began to fail him in typical "old dog" ways, but he still managed to find his way around the Pulley property with the help of his friend, Georgette, who literally got in front of him and guided him when he headed in the wrong direction. He lost most of his teeth, spent much of his time sleeping, got confused about where he was sometimes, and his kidneys started to fail. His eyes became a real issue because the pressure in his eyes wasn't good, and Bear began to experience pain. Judy was open to removing Bear's eyes so he would be more comfortable, but tests revealed that the kidney failure, which had previously been in early stages, had escalated and after four years with Judy it was time for Bear to leave his body.

Judy says, "It was the hardest decision I have ever had to make and for a long time I second guessed myself. My vet told me more than once, 'It may not have been the right decision for you, but it was for him.'"

When Judy thinks about what Bear taught her she immediately responds with a lesson about "limitations and not feeling sorry for ourselves when our lives don't go as planned." She adds, "Some people shy away from dogs that

are blind or old, but Bear showed us that dogs can quickly adapt to new environments. Having a dog with a disability is a real inspiration and nothing to be concerned about. What an inspiration to us old people who find ourselves feeling sorry for ourselves when we have aches and pains. Actually, because of knowing Little Sir Gruntly Bear, my daughter and her husband have adopted a dog with eye issues as well as a puppy mill dog. I'm very proud of them.

"I will never forget him and will always, always miss him no matter how many dogs I love."

Judy will be paying it forward soon when she retires. Because of her experience with Bear she "would like to provide a Final Refuge home for Old Dog Haven. No one I know understands why I would want to do that (except my daughter and son-in-law) and although I understand why most people don't get it, I can't figure out why someone wouldn't want to be that person who gives some old soul a great final ending, no matter how long that is."

Good for you, Judy. I'm sure that Bear has sent out the word and before you know it, you'll have more old dogs lined up, wanting to spend their final time here with you.

I should also add that during the time Bear was with Judy she provided pictures and updates to Peggi Engstrom and her children. When Peggi died, her daughter sent Judy an email thanking her for "giving Mom's Bear such a good home. I printed out one of the pictures you sent of Bear and put it up on her wall, and that picture was laid to rest with her today. She spoke of Bear often, right up to the very last thing she said to me as I walked out of her hospital room one night. After I said good-bye she responded with 'Leave Bear here.' I assured her he was right next to her."

Isn't it wonderful how one little dog was capable of generating so much love with the people and animals who cared about him?

EMILY

"She was one of a kind."

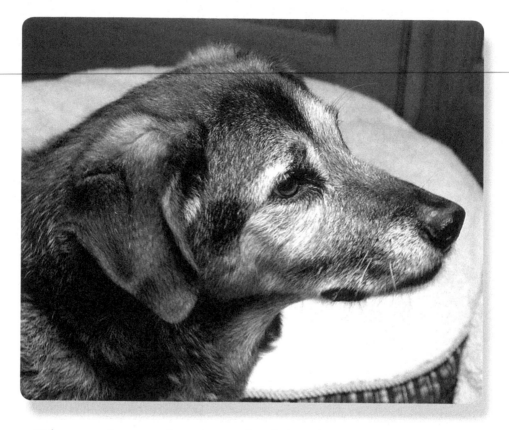

When people surrender a dog to the shelter they give all kinds of reasons why the dog is no longer welcome in their home. One of the most common excuses given by people is that they no longer have time for the dog. This rationalization is particularly common when an older dog is brought to the shelter. In some cases, a more honest statement might be: "The dog is old and we don't want to take care of her any longer."

But, people aren't always honest about why they're bringing a dog to the shelter. Sometimes they just want someone else to assume responsibility for the dog.

Take Emily, for example. Emily was adopted from a local shelter when she was a puppy. Ten years later she was returned to the same shelter by the people who had adopted her because the family "didn't have time for her."

We found two people who did have time for Emily. Priscilla and Bryan McCarty were happy to welcome Emily into their home and hearts. Emily lived happily with Priscilla and Bryan for two years and they loved her ev-

38

ery moment she spent with them. Here's Emily's story, beautifully narrated by Priscilla:

"Can you imagine how it must have felt to this dear old soul who suddenly found herself in a shelter after years of living in a home with a family? We couldn't imagine how frightening that must have felt, and so, when Old Dog Haven contacted us, we went to meet her right away. Emily seemed a bit withdrawn at first, and didn't even respond to us with a wag of her tail. But her beautiful eyes said 'Please take me home with you and love me.' How could we resist?

"Even though she was very quiet when we brought her here, it was obvious that she and my husband bonded immediately. We were told at the shelter that she had been raised with two boys so it seemed she identified with males because of those memories. She must have had wonderful times with those boys and felt like my husband was made of the 'same stuff.'

"We live on a five acre farm with horses, a donkey, chickens, other Final Refuge dogs from Old Dog Haven and one bossy cat! It didn't appear that Emily had ever seen a horse or donkey before, and she was extra cautious around them. She watched the chickens with interest, but it was as if she knew she should never bother them and she never did. Not the same for the cat! She took great delight in pestering the cat, but not ever in a mean way. Because of her (mostly) German shepherd background, she was bigger than any of the other dogs we had living with us, but she was always very respectful and never used her size to intimidate anyone or anything. We don't feel she had one mean bone in her body.

"While living here, Emily's favorite thing was to follow my husband anywhere he went, whether it was outside, in the barn, or over to his shop, where she had her own bed and always kept a watchful eye on him. She loved to ride with him in his truck too, and all he had to do was to ask her if she wanted to go, and she was up and ready at a moment's notice! As time went on, it became harder for her to get into the truck, but she was always more than willing to wait patiently until my husband could give her a 'boost' up into the seat, where she would ride happily next to him until it was time to head for home.

"She was excellent around our grandchildren, and was always patient and polite with any 'new' dog that came to visit or to live here. We knew we could always trust her to be kind to everyone. She never let us down.

"Emily learned how to 'shake' for a cookie shortly after arriving here, and if you ever wanted to get her attention, all you had to say was 'cookie' and she was on her feet and headed toward you. Her other favorite treat was the small end of the carrots we had in the barn for the horses. They were tiny pieces, but she could catch that carrot as if it were a piece of steak. And eat it with that much gusto too.

"As time went on, it was harder for her to get around, but every day when the rest of us went for our afternoon or evening walk, Emily would sit at the back door of the barn and wait for us to come back to her. We are sure she was saying (with those beautiful brown eyes) that she didn't want us to worry; she would be right there when we returned. And she always was.

"We called Emily the 'Grand Dame' of the dogs we had living here because she always acted as if it was her job to watch over everyone else. One of our other Final Refuge dogs loved to come up and kiss Emily on the mouth. It was obvious that Emily really didn't enjoy this, but she would tolerate the kisses rather than being rude and walking away. Another of our other Final Refuge dogs, Sadie, is totally deaf, and doesn't always pay attention to where the other dogs are sitting, but if Sadie stepped on Emily, it was as if Emily would look at Sadie and say, 'I know you didn't know I was sitting right next to you and I am not mad at you for stepping on me.'

"I think my husband and I would both say that three of the many things we loved about Emily were that she totally accepted everyone for just who they were, that good behavior was a trait she always wanted to exhibit, and that unconditional love just came naturally to her. A lesson we humans could practice too!

"Sadly, the last week of January 2012, we lost dear Emily, after her liver began to fail, and her arthritis was making it almost impossible for her to get around.

"My husband and I both often wondered how anyone could have taken this beautiful dog back to the shelter because we believe she must have given them unconditional love just like she did us. If anyone ever wants to know what unconditional love really feels like, we highly recommend you consider giving an old dog a new home with you! We know you will not be sorry. We wouldn't trade the experience for anything and believe that these loving old dogs deserve a wonderful home until the day they pass on. We only hope Emily felt we showed her as much love as she shared with us every single day she lived here. We were blessed and honored to call her 'our dog' and will never forget her time here."

Priscilla wrote the above narrative about Emily just days after she and Bryan had to release her from her body. And, less than a week after Emily physically left them, these two kind and caring people were ready to welcome another old dog into their home. They were looking forward to meeting their new girl, but Emily will never be forgotten by the two people who not only did have time for her, but loved her and learned many important lessons from her.

"We'll always have a special place in our hearts for Em. She was one of a kind."

BO

"People remembered him when they came to visit."

I first met Bo in late 2005, when Judith asked me to visit him in his home and to meet the woman who had called about the possibility of Old Dog Haven taking him. When the door to the apartment opened, I was greeted by a young woman and a dog that looked as though he'd been dipped in leather. Bo only had hair on the top of his head, at the end of his tail, and along his spine. He was clearly suffering from the worst yeast infection I'd ever seen. He was also painfully thin. Emaciated.

I wanted to take Bo with me right then, but the woman was having a very hard time giving him up because her young son loved him—as did she—and she was still struggling with the idea of surrendering him to Old Dog Haven. She hadn't treated his skin condition, she knew that he needed more care than she could provide, and she was moving. But still … he was her dog. She cared about him but hadn't been caring for him. She needed more time. I told her that I understood, but I was concerned about Bo's physical condition and asked her to think hard about what was best for him. She promised to do that and said she'd call Judith soon.

About two weeks later, she did call. She was ready to surrender Bo to Old Dog Haven. Lee picked him up and in January 2006 Bo became a permanent resident at Home Base.

Bo's skin needed immediate attention so Judith and Lee began a specially designed rehab program for Bo. With proper diet and medication, his coat eventually became silky and actually fluffy. Bo's weight—he only weighed forty-eight pounds when he came to Home Base—also needed serious attention. By the time he left, almost two years later, he weighed eighty-five pounds and looked like a handsome representative of the Newfoundland breed. (He was actually probably a mix of Newfoundland and something else.) He looked beautiful after his skin cleared up and he gained weight.

There's a tree farm not far from Home Base and Bo was no different from the other dogs that are able to do the walk at the tree farm; he loved it. His favorite thing to do on the trail was to play hide and seek with Judith and Lee. He never stayed hidden for long though; he wanted to be found.

Judith was concerned about Bo not having a young boy to play with at Home Base so when kids came to visit she made sure that they spent time with Bo. Actually, it wasn't even necessary for her to orchestrate Bo's kid visits; kids loved him, and any kids who came to Home Base immediately gravitated to him and he to them. In general, Bo was a dog that people—regardless of age—remembered when they came to visit.

Judith says that it was really "fun to watch him turn into a healthy dog. We learned a lot from Bo about how to treat yeast infections."

Bo was a tough-guy-wanna-be. He had a big bark and he looked fierce, but his tough guy image was always spoiled by the sight of his tail wagging back and forth as fast as it could rotate. His smile always gave him away too. Judith sums Bo's personality up very well when she says he was "a very cool dog."

Almost two years after Bo arrived at Home Base his body failed him. A tumor had been found at the base of his heart. Even though he did fine for several months, the tumor finally began to impede his breathing, and Judith and Lee had to release him from his body. Judith says, "He hung on with a smile on that wonderful face as long as he could. We miss him greatly."

I should add a note here about Bo's family. In contrast to most people who surrender dogs to Old Haven and never maintain contact, Bo's lady kept in touch with Judith and Lee during the entire time Bo was with them. She even sent money from time to time to help pay for his care, which is quite unusual, and was very much appreciated.

It was my pleasure to have known Bo and to have spent time with him on occasion when I went to Home Base. I loved touching him and feeling his soft fur, which was such a contrast to the leathery skin he had when I first met him.

One of my favorite images of Bo was seeing him lounging on the couch with his head draped over the back so he could look out the window. It was wonderful to watch him become healthy and secure. He was a very well loved dog and he knew it. What a guy!

OZZIE

Taking Care of Each Other

In the second chapter, I said that Old Dog Haven looks like an organization on the surface, but really is a family. Our efforts, as are those of successful families, are always team efforts aimed at giving old dogs a second chance at happiness.

The concept of Old Dog Haven as a family of people who help old dogs is beautifully illustrated in the story of Ozzie. Saving Ozzie was truly a team effort: Judith made it happen; Heidi Espe was his foster mom and initial rehab coach for several months; Alicia Kobory went above and beyond to fix his coat and skin. And, finally, Kathy Jackson (Mc Elheny) became his Final Refuge mom and partner for almost four years, assisted in his physical care by Old Dog Haven volunteer, Diane Haviland. Here's how it all played out:

Judith received a call from a pastor who was very concerned about an old dog living with one of his parishioners who would soon be leaving town. Judith agreed to take the dog (Ozzie) and arrangements were made for Judith to pick him up in Monroe because Ozzie's human friend didn't have enough gas to drive more than a few miles.

Judith remembers the trip home very well. "I've never smelled anything like Ozzie. His skin and ears were infected with yeast, filth, cigarette smoke—who knows what else. He was a wreck, but we could tell he was an unusually charismatic dog.

"It took nearly two months of hard work from Heidi, as well as many vet visits, to get him over the worst of it. Meanwhile, our wonderful groomer, Alicia, made time for him on a regular basis, to help his skin and coat start to recover.

"When I heard from an older lady who wanted to take in a Final Refuge senior dog, she had some specific criteria. The new addition to her family needed to be big enough to protect her and well behaved enough to handle long walks. Ozzie seemed the perfect choice. And he was!"

Heidi Espe, Ozzie's foster mom, also remembers Ozzie with great affection: "Ozzie was a great dog who, despite all of his physical neglect, still loved and trusted people. On that first car trip to my home, he smelled so awful I had to roll all the windows down. He just looked at me from the back seat with those trusting brown eyes. The aroma in my car became even more interesting when he threw up, which also happened in Judith's car. Upset stomach aside, he immediately fit right into the routine of things, running around with his tongue hanging out and romping around in the heavy snow trying to find the ball. Ozzie was one of the sweetest, kindest, and most well-mannered companions I've ever fostered. Everyone he came in contact with fell in love with him."

And then there's Alicia Kobory, Ozzie's groomer. Alicia says, "Ozzie was the coolest dog in the world. I've been in this business a long time and have seen one or two dogs that I felt lucky to meet. Ozzie is one of them. He came in with half the hair he should have had and several bald spots. He was an old dog who thought he was a puppy, and desperately wanted to be a lap dog, even with his 90ish pound body. Anyone who got to know him is the luckiest person around. He picked up on your strengths and weaknesses and did everything he could to help.

"His Final Refuge mom, Kathy, did everything she could for him. The first time I saw the two of them together they were walking down our gravel path with its occasional rough spots. She had some trouble and he stayed right by her side, preventing her from falling. I think they both had a job. She's a woman who was helping a dog rehabilitate and he went out of his way to be her therapist. After a grooming session, when she came to pick him up, he did his crazy happy stuff but never jumped on her. Once, when he hit her with his tail accidentally, he turned around right away to see if she was okay.

Kathy Jackson also remembers Ozzie with love and gratitude: "The main thing about Ozzie was that he was so good! He always tried to do what was expected of him and he was so smart that he understood right away. When I decided that it was bedtime, he went into the bedroom and slept on his bed, which was on the floor right beside mine. He never woke or bothered me, except for one day when I slept much later than usual and he came over to check on me. He put his nose right up against my face. I didn't even mind that he woke me up because it just meant that someone cared about me.

"You've never seen a hungrier dog than Ozzie. He loved to eat, and I loved to feed him. He loved the dog biscuits I baked for him. When Ozzie first came to me, he had some physical ailments that kept him from feeling altogether well, and I also had a bad knee that needed surgery. After he felt better and my knee had been repaired we went for long walks together, and we both enjoyed that a lot. We also went to the dog park where he could rough and tumble with many other dogs while I sat on a log. I am so thankful to have had this wonderful dog and believe he was happy to live with me."

I also have a memory of Ozzie that I'd like to share with you. I met Ozzie once at an Old Dog Haven picnic that he attended with Kathy. In fact, I went to the picnic specifically to meet Ozzie because I'd seen his photo on the website and I'd heard so much about him. When I arrived at the park, I looked around to see if I could locate Ozzie and Kathy, and there they were, sitting under the pavilion. Kathy was seated at a table, and Ozzie was lying on a blanket at her feet. When I told Kathy that I'd come to meet Ozzie, she instantly put her hand on his head and began to tell me about him. There was such love in her voice as she spoke about her friend, and I could see in Ozzie's eyes that her love was returned as he listened to her. Before I knew it, I was sitting on the blanket with Ozzie; I couldn't keep my hands off of him either. He was very gracious with me, but his interest was clearly focused on his mom. They were devoted to each other, and I loved seeing that exchange of emotion. I feel very fortunate to have met Ozzie that day because it wasn't long after the picnic that Ozzie's body failed him and he physically had to leave this life.

After nearly four years with Kathy, Ozzie succumbed suddenly to a large tumor around his heart. It was so like Ozzie that he hid any problem from his many admirers until the last moment. It took a huge tumor to overcome his wonderfully strong heart.

Ozzie was such a good friend to his mom as well as a fabulous ambassador for Old Dog Haven. He was so loved by many, and I'm absolutely sure Ozzie is smiling as we remember him and is feeling good about doing his job so well during the time he lived with Kathy.

HIS NAME WAS FRANK

*"He was not a puppy mill dog when he left us. He was OUR dog;
a loved dog, a bed-partner, a buddy."*

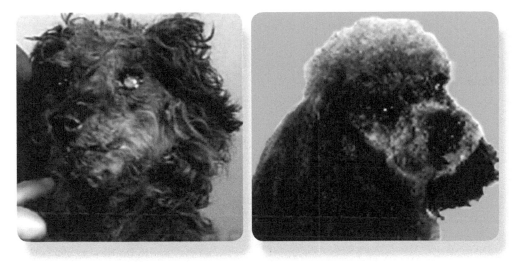

Frank on the day he was rescued   *Frank one year later*

I don't know how much you know about puppy mills, but let me take a little space here to give you some information about them before we get to Frank's story. I could talk about puppy mills for many pages, but that's a subject for someone else's book, so I'll just cut to the chase and give you some basic facts:

Puppy mills are breeding factories that employ inhumane tactics to produce puppies for profit.

Puppy mill breeder dogs live their entire lives in unlined, wire cages, often stacked one on top of the other so that the urine and feces from above drips down into the cages below. These animals receive little or no human contact, inadequate nutrition, no veterinary care, and no exercise. These horrible conditions promote diseases which can be passed on to the other animals, painful injuries which often go untreated, and even birth defects and deformities from over-breeding and in-breeding.

Female dogs are usually bred continuously from their first heat cycle until they can no longer produce any more puppies. After a litter is born, the puppies are taken from their mother before being properly weaned and sold, primarily to pet stores—about 90% of puppies sold in pet stores originate from puppy mills and through the Internet.

According to the American Humane Society there are an estimated 10,000 puppy mills in the U.S. They produce approximately one million puppies a year.

In 2010, the Office of the Inspector General released a report detailing the United States Department of Agriculture's (USDA) lax and ineffective enforcement of the Animal Welfare Act (AWA) against licensed large-scale dog breeders and brokers known as puppy mills. As part of the investigation, auditors visited eighty-one facilities and reviewed records documenting 28,443 violations over a two-year period.

The report concludes that despite regular inspections, breeders were allowed to continue operating facilities where dogs lived in inhumane conditions—cages overflowing with pools of urine and feces, food laden with dead cockroaches, and dogs infested with ticks and unattended injuries including a mutilated leg and other atrocities—all without penalty. Furthermore, in cases of severe neglect and abuse, inspectors failed to confiscate the animals. At one Oklahoma mill, despite discovering five dead dogs and others that had resorted to cannibalism due to starvation, investigators took no action, which resulted in the deaths of twenty-two more dogs.

The ASPCA has been painfully aware of the cruel conditions to which dogs are regularly subjected at the hands of puppy mill operators who put profit above providing the most basic standards of care. "Puppy mills are a primary focus of the ASPCA's anti-cruelty initiatives," says Cori Menkin, ASPCA Senior Director of Legislative Initiatives. "While the ASPCA commends the Office of the Inspector General for its detailed audit, we hope the findings will lead to stronger, more consistent enforcement by the USDA, more federal funding to increase the number of inspectors enforcing the Animal Welfare Act, and ultimately, more humane conditions for the dogs." Because many puppy mills now sell directly to consumers over the Internet, they escape the minimal USDA standards that apply to breeders who sell to pet stores. "It's a massive loophole," says USDA spokesperson, Jessica Milteer.

Authorities rescued dogs from puppy mills in the United States an average of every four and a half days in 2011. That's a record, but there are still many puppy mills operating under the radar and current legislation still isn't strong enough to put all puppy mills out of business. I hope that in time these horrible places will cease to exist, but that can only happen through stronger legislation, enforcement of local laws and ordinances, and a refusal on the part of pet stores to buy dogs from puppy mills.

Thankfully, current research indicates that a ray of hope is emerging about pet stores and puppy mills. Many pet stores are now forming partnerships with shelters and are no longer buying dogs from puppy mills. The ASPCA has issued a positive statement supporting the idea of pet stores selling rescue animals as long as they meet specific criteria.

In January 2009, investigators in Mount Vernon, Washington raided one of the largest puppy mill operations in state history. They found close to 400 animals. Many of the dogs were sick, existing in filthy cages, with insufficient food and water. Days later, a similar raid in Snohomish County (of a site linked to the Mount Vernon business) revealed another 200 animals. Many of the dogs were pregnant, so not only did the adult and senior dogs need care, but puppies would soon arrive that also needed care and nurturing.

Rescue organizations, including Old Dog Haven, were contacted and the arduous task of helping the dogs began. Among the 600 dogs rescued was Frank, and this is his story. Except for interrupting now and then with editorial comments, I'm going to let the woman who loved Frank tell you about him in her own way because Robyn Miller saw Frank as more than just a puppy mill survivor, and it was she and her husband, Ken, who gave Frank an opportunity to be a real dog during the time he lived with them. Here's Frank's story as told by Robyn Miller:

"I'm going to start at the end and save you the dread of waiting to find out what eventually happens to Frank. I start his story within days of the third anniversary of seeing Frank for the first time during his courageous and long-over due rescue, and five months after our tearful good-bye.

"After you've had an old dog for over a year or so, you are lulled into the false sense that they will live forever. So it was a normal day, a beautiful low-stress Saturday in August, but Frank didn't want to eat his breakfast, and he was throwing up ... not at all like Frank. He ate anything and everything and had a rock in his stomach to prove it. After a call to Chuckanut Valley Veterinary Animal Hospital that morning asking what they thought, we headed in to see what he had eaten this time. They asked us to leave him so they could check him out and run some tests, but it didn't feel right leaving him. He hated being separated from me and would get so scared. But, we did reluctantly leave him for the tests.

"You too may have received one of these calls where you're not really sure what is being said at the other end of the line and your mind goes into a fog. You try to keep your wits about you so you can talk somewhat intelligently. This was one of those calls. Frank was in liver failure.

"We brought him home, let him do what he enjoyed the most, sitting on my lap, and just loved on him remembering why we took him in, why we loved him so much, and why he was so special. The next day he found peace, never to be afraid or nervous again, being held and soothed by those who loved him most, his people.

Full Circle

"Inauguration, January 21, 2009, was an exciting day. We sat in freezing cold but sunny weather in Washington D.C. witnessing history at the swearing in of our 44th President. Rescuing a very old poodle was the farthest thing from our minds, especially my husband's!

"When we returned home I received a call from a fellow rescuer and Old Dog Haven foster home provider who was in attendance at the puppy mill raid where over 400 dogs were eventually taken in. She took Frank home that first night because no would take him and he needed to be out of the chaos. The need was so great for so many, but Frank was old—determined to be twelve-fourteen years—still being used for breeding, and not puppy cute. She called to see if we would take him; he needed a safe, quiet place to heal emotionally.

"We learned the details of Frank's rescue from Old Dog Haven and SPOT (Saving Pets One at a Time) volunteer, Jen Sevigny. Frank was taken during the first raid of a large Skagit County puppy mill. He was living in a two feet by three feet wire cage with a female gray poodle, and he was whining and covered in feces. When Frank was removed from the cage, his eyes weren't visible because the hair was matted over them and knotted all the way to his mouth. Rescuers suspected he was old, but did not realize how old until they checked his teeth. Frank spent some time at the Skagit Valley Fairgrounds in a barn type building that the sheriff's deputies and local firemen were trying to figure out how to heat safely. Because Frank was in such poor condition, it was determined that he needed a foster family immediately. Before we picked him up, Jen and other volunteer rescuers managed to clean his face a bit and snip some of the hair from his eyes before putting him in his own travel crate.

"How could I say no when others were doing so much? We have never had a poodle, let alone a small poodle. It conjures up images that just aren't us. We have a golden retriever! Not a purse dog!

"When we went to the rescue staging location, they took Frank out of the carrier for us to see. He had to be shaved to the skin because he was so matted and dirty. They thought he was a brown poodle, not a silver/black, because he was so filthy, dirty. And he was skinny … skin hanging on bones. (A fat content of one out of four.) He had a mature cataract in one eye, no teeth, part of his lower jaw was missing due to a previous infection, and he was partially debarked. But, other than that, he was in pretty good health; you just wouldn't know it to look at him.

"If you've ever taken in a dog, rescue or otherwise, you know that once you see them face-to-face, you don't walk away. So off we went, with our purse-size poodle.

I need to back up a little and say that I said yes to taking in another dog, but I didn't ask my husband, Ken. When I told him about saying yes, while he didn't say no, he didn't say anything at all. For two days.

"When Frank came home, I set him up in his own area, very comfortable by dog standards, but he quickly started to cry. Strange I thought for a dog that was used to not having people around. And it wasn't going to make any points with Ken. So, I went and got him. I wanted to put him in bed with us, but I didn't want to push my luck. So, I did what any understanding-dog-rescuing wife would do; I slept on the couch with the dog. And that's when he melted my heart. He snuggled down next to me and didn't move or whimper all night long. I was his safe harbor. He trusted me.

"As winter also melted into spring and Frank put on a few healthy pounds, we were faced with determining if he was adoptable or not. We felt he would do better with someone who was home all day with him, preferably a woman, because he was afraid of men, especially when they walked up to him. Even Ken. And he wouldn't let strangers pick him up.

"So we posted him up for adoption on the infamous and addicting Old Dog Haven website. Even though Frank was rescued through SPOT, his care was transferred to Old Dog Haven due to his age and the vast numbers of animals in SPOT's care at the time. A wonderful example of rescue groups teaming together for the common good of animals. Within a few days we had a single, retired woman interested in adopting Frank. We had to put his best interests before our emotional attachment to him, so we decided that would be the best placement.

"My husband takes our golden retriever, Lucy, out for a walk every morning. The morning we were taking Frank to his new home, Ken took Lucy for the walk only to return shortly after he left, tearfully proclaiming that he didn't want Frank to go to another home. He didn't think Frank would do well separated from me, so Frank settled in to stay.

"Frank went everywhere with us. Because he wanted to, we wanted him to, and because he had a hard time with strangers. Frank slept with us, both of us, from that 'second' night! In bed, he wasn't afraid of Ken. He loved to travel, especially long-car rides. He made two trips to California and numerous trips to Spokane and Centralia, sleeping on my lap the whole way.

"He became a spokes-dog for the puppy mill rescue, visiting schools in his custom made jacket, and retirement centers where residents would share stories of dogs they knew. On Frank's last visit to the Country Meadow Retirement Center, an elderly gentleman in a wheel chair came up and began to talk about a little poodle that he had befriended during the war in France. He then asked us if he could pet Frank. As he was petting him, I asked if he had ever had a poodle after the war, and he said he had never had a dog. I was later told that this man had never attended a social function in the center until that day."

I need to interrupt Robyn's narrative about Frank for a couple of paragraphs to give an "atta girl" to former 8th grade Shuksan Middle School teacher Staci Hurley, and to let Staci tell you about Frank's visits to her school.

Staci says, "I elected to teach a Humane Education unit focusing on the pet overpopulation problem and the factors that contribute to it. Students learned about responsible pet ownership, which includes choosing the right type of animal for your family, making a commitment to the animal for its entire life-time, the importance of exercise and positive training, and making that animal an integral part of the family.

"Students also learned about the importance of spaying and neutering their own pets and being part of the solution rather than part of the problem. The Spay Station visited our school and the students had the chance to tour it.

"Students also watched videos that showed the reality of what goes on in shelters across the United States every single day. I felt like it was easy for them to distance themselves from the problem when they just hear a number, but when you watch a healthy, loving animal be put down for no reason other than overcrowding in shelters, it really sends the message home.

"Students read about puppy mills and saw photos and watched footage of dogs living in deplorable conditions in cages, but again, I felt if we could put a real life face to that suffering, it would be a much more powerful message for them. I wanted them to meet Frank and understand that he is just like any of their pets and just as deserving of a loving home. I wanted them to imagine their dog living in a wire cage and never setting foot on solid ground or never knowing human kindness. I wanted to convey to them that they have the power to stop this; they can choose to adopt an animal from a shelter or rescue group and not buy one off of the Internet or from a pet store, they can educate other people about what they have learned, or they can use their vote when they turn eighteen to help change the laws. By having Frank and Robyn come to class, the students got to hear firsthand what these animals endured and also see the amazing spirit and resiliency of these dogs that are so forgiving and re-ally just want to love and be loved.

"Frank became a bit of a superstar amongst the 8th graders. Since he came to visit six times, kids who had met him in previous sessions would see him in the hall and rush up to pet him. You would hear them running to friends to tell them, 'Frank is here! Let's go see him!' The students would always ask why Frank's tongue was sticking out (Robyn's most favorite Frank characteristic) and she would tell them … 'because he doesn't have any teeth.' You could just see their minds trying to figure out the reasoning for that.

"I don't know how much Frank liked being in the limelight, but he was a good sport and an excellent ambassador for puppy mill survivors. Robyn did a great job of educating the students and sharing Frank's experience and his impact on her life. She did a presentation that included photos from the raid and showed Frank's journey during his first year with his new family.

"My main goal in all of this was to educate my students so that they can make informed choices in the future. Many of them didn't realize we had low cost spay/neuter options or how allowing their dog to have even one litter contributes to the overpopulation problem and results in healthy animals being euthanized in shelters. Others had no idea about puppy mills and how many are in our own backyard right here in Washington and how by buying a puppy off of the Internet or at a pet store, they are supporting the puppy mill industry and the suffering of more dogs."

Frank, Robyn and Shuksan Middle School students

Staci has since moved to another state, but is hopefully continuing her crusade to educate young people about puppy mills and other animal welfare issues. Okay, now back to Robyn's story about Frank.

"The old boy didn't have much expression. It was hard to know what he was thinking most of the time, but there was no mistaking his joy when my car would pull into the driveway or I would walk into the house. He had a spring to his step that he had been saving up all day, just for me. Ken said Frank would sit at the back door and look out, waiting. On nice days he was at the fence peering out with his 'good eye' as I pulled in the driveway. He'd start jumping and hopping around, just waiting for me to pick him up and give the familiar, 'Hey buddy.'

"He learned to tolerate Ken. Even though Ken worked so hard to get him to 'love' him, even feeding him by hand didn't quite seal the deal. Later we learned the 'care givers' of the puppy mill were men. Loud, rough, unkind men who see these small dogs as profit makers.

"Who knows how long Frank had been caged. I can't help but think that at some point Frank had been someone's pet, living in a house and loved. How do you learn to love and trust so quickly if you've never experienced it? What must he have thought and felt when he was first put in a cage? Never to be groomed, brushed, or properly fed. I try not to think about that part. How lucky for us too that he was rescued, for he taught us patience, compassion, trust, and to slow down the pace.

"Frank's legacy is not being a puppy mill survivor. It's about a new beginning and purpose no matter what age or size. He was not a puppy mill dog when he left us; he was our dog, a loved dog, a bed-partner, a buddy, and his name was Frank!

Frank and Robyn

Frank's friends were many:

- "Old Dog Haven and SPOT volunteers saw him as a testament to all their efforts and dedication to all rescued animals.
- Jen & Mike Sevigny: His true rescuers and heroes, who he loved to give the 'stink eye.'
- Sandy, his groomer, who first shaved Frank to the skin and nicknamed him Bear, because they thought he was brown.
- Chuckanut Valley Veterinary Clinic where Frank was taken such good care of and welcomed at each visit.
- Residents of Country Meadow Retirement Center where Frank would visit as a representative of ODH and SPOT, 'helping' the senior volunteers do animal rescue paperwork.
- Shuksan Middle School staff and students, whom Frank would visit and tell his rescue story, to remind them that every animal, young, old, big, or small has value and a purpose.
- Niece Berit, who saw past Frank's exterior and loved him unconditionally.
- His cat Violet: She loved Frank. It was hard to get a read on how Frank felt about her.
- Mike & CeCe: The neighbors who welcomed him into their home at each visit.
- The Family who loved Frank because we did. Thank you.

Epilogue

"A month after we lost Frank, we took in another small, old poodle, a cast off from a breeder rescued by Old Dog Haven. Bennie was ten years old, with no hair on his back or bottom. He was a sweetie pie, and he liked Ken. Bennie did find a forever adoptive home in January. He wasn't Frank; he was his own dog, but we have had to admit, we love small poodles! Our home consists of our 12-year-old golden, Lucy, and another of the puppy mill 'puppies' Lilly, a West Highland White Terrier that would have had a very painful life as a breeding female because she has had multiple structural issues in her three short years. Our poodle rescue days are not over; we talk about saying 'yes' again, when I am home all day. We know Frank would chuckle at the thought of making us poodle people!

"If you have never said 'yes' to an old dog, please consider it. They have so much left to give and teach us, just when we think we are rescuing them. Thank you for caring."

A final note: Frank wasn't the only senior dog taken in by Old Dog Haven from the puppy mill raids in 2009. Old Dog Haven took in a total of twenty senior dogs from four different raids within a very short period of time. Four of the dogs stayed in our Final Refuge homes and sixteen of them were adopted.

Our foster parents deserve tremendous credit for the great job they did in turning these terrified, filthy creatures, mostly no longer housebroken, into fairly confident, happy dogs that were able to join new families.

One of the puppy mill owners was convicted of animal neglect and abuse in 2010, but she continued to contest forfeiting the dogs. Her particular case dragged on until March 2012, when finally the dogs were declared officially free. They were all safe during this waiting period, thanks to SPOT and Old Dog Haven, but now they're actually free.

Daisy, the last dog to be free, had been fostered by Eric and Mary Sommers since 2009. These patient people didn't really know about Old Dog Haven back in 2009, but they innocently volunteered to foster a puppy mill dog, never dreaming that the legal status of Daisy would take so long to resolve. How did Eric and Mary react to the news that Daisy was finally free? They officially adopted her.

ELLIE

"She became one of our joys in doing what we do."

You probably can't imagine giving up your canine companion after the dog has been with you for thirteen years, can you? Yet, some people are able to do this without any regrets. I'm not talking here about people who become ill and are no longer able to care for their dogs. I'm talking about people who bring their dogs to shelters because they don't want the dogs any longer. All sorts of reasons are always given, as I've mentioned before, but the bottom line is always the same: the person surrendering the dog would like someone else to assume responsibility for the dog.

Ellie was thirteen when she was brought to The Humane Society for Tacoma and Pierce County by the only human companion she'd ever known. The woman who surrendered Ellie said she kept "escaping from the yard" and she didn't want to deal with her any longer. This was in 2005 when Old Dog Haven was just getting started and the shelter's Volunteer Rescue Coordinators, Erica Stewart and Sandy Nelson, had just become aware of Old Dog Haven. Erica called Judith, who agreed to take Ellie. Because Erica had never met Judith and really didn't know anything about this new and unusual rescue group, she and Sandy volunteered to drive Ellie to Arlington. Judith and Lee clearly passed Erica's "let's check these people out" test because four days later Erica called them about another old dog needing a home. To this date, Old Dog Haven has taken in more dogs from the Tacoma shelter than any other shelter in western Washington, primarily due to the Rescue Volunteers' efforts and excellent vet reports.

Physically, Ellie was very thin and had ruptured ligaments in both knees and a large, fatty tumor. Her lungs were typical "old dog lungs."

But physical issues weren't the major concern with Ellie. When she first arrived at Home Base, Ellie didn't trust anyone. Judith says, "She had a shell around her for a long time and a big chip on her shoulder. She was standoffish to some extent, mostly because no one had given her a reason not to be. She was clearly grieving for the loss of her person. It took months for her to gain weight, to get over the grief, to trust us and accept living in a big group. When she finally felt secure, she became one of our joys in doing what we do."

Judith remembers that joy manifesting itself in a dramatic way one day after Ellie had been with them for several months. This experience was a really big deal! Judith was out in the pasture with the dogs and Ellie was off by herself exploring one end of the field. Judith called to her and something must have clicked because Ellie came running to her with a big smile on her face. Her gait was awkward because of her knees, but enthusiasm was clearly there for the first time. Judith gave her a big hug, which she accepted graciously with a serious tail wag, and from that day forward the trust that Judith and Lee were so hoping would eventually be there between them and Ellie was forged in steel.

A general comment here relevant to the experience I've just described: Judith and Lee have taken in many dogs over the years and they've learned, thanks to Ellie initially, that "you can't fuss over or smother a new dog. Gaining their trust usually takes time. You can't have expectations, and you can't force yourself on a dog."

As time passed, Ellie settled in and became one of the gang. She actually wanted to be the alpha female, but Queenie, whom you'll meet later, had that role nailed down, so Ellie eventually settled for #2 alpha, wisely conceding that she was outweighed and out-determined by Queenie.

Never once did Ellie try to escape from the yard. She grew to love her home, especially the pasture. Judith says that Ellie reinforced the idea that "this place and being out and moving around helps them physically." She had a habit of burying her dog bones vertically, maybe because they were easier to find that way. Who knows? Lee tried to avoid them, but ended up running over them with the mower, much to Ellie's dismay. To this day Lee still finds Ellie's bones in the pasture.

Ellie loved kids. It's unknown whether she had lived with children and was used to them, or whether she just liked their energy, but when kids came to Home Base to visit the dogs, Ellie was always front and center ready to spend time with them.

After two years with Judith and Lee, Ellie began to slow down and her ruptured knee ligaments and old dog lungs limited her walks. The struggle to breathe and make those stiff old legs work became just too difficult for her. She tried hard to keep up with everyone, but it was just too much.

Judith says, "There was a hole in our home and our hearts when Ellie left. It's an incredible compliment to Ellie that she would decide people are okay after being abandoned as she was. Humans can't do that. She was a very cool dog."

AARON

"He will be missed for all of my life."

An estimated 250,000 animals are victims of animal hoarding each year. This abuse differs from other types of animal cruelty in that hoarders don't always accept or recognize the cruelty they inflict on their animals. Rather, animal hoarders usually believe they are saving or rescuing the animals they imprison. Animals kept in hoarding conditions often suffer extreme neglect, including lack of food, proper veterinary care and sanitary conditions.

Records kept by ALDF (Animal Legal Defense Fund) indicate that in the last four years the number of reported hoarding cases has more than doubled. In terms of the number of animals affected and the degree and duration of their suffering, hoarding is the number one animal cruelty crisis facing companion animals in communities throughout the country.

Many states have no legal definition for animal hoarding. Courts already assign relatively low priority to animal abuse and neglect cases in general, and many people are unfamiliar with the severity of abuse in hoarding situations. The high cost of caring for animals rescued from hoarders often must be paid by rescuers and is also a huge disincentive for prosecuting hoarding cases. These factors contribute to a lengthy and difficult legal process in securing a positive verdict in any case.

In 2009, Animal Control officers arrived at a home near Seattle because they had received complaints that animals were allegedly being housed in unsanitary conditions. Twenty-two dogs were found living in conditions that defy description. One year later, thirty-eight dogs were taken from the same hoarder. All sixty of the dogs spent time at animal shelters while the legal process churned away. Old Dog Haven was asked to take the senior dogs on both occasions, and we agreed to place them in our family network of homes after they were officially released to us.

Aaron, a sheltie about twelve years old, was among the thirty-eight dogs confiscated in 2010. After spending two weeks in a shelter, one of our long-time foster/Final Refuge moms (who prefers to only be known as Linda) brought Aaron home to live with her. Linda knew she would only be providing short term hospice care for Aaron because he was in terrible shape, but she was happy to have him with her even for a short period of time.

Aaron came with a very serious case of giardia, causing violent diarrhea. He also had a large inoperable tumor in his rectum, causing him great pain. He had clearly been suffering for a very long time.

Interestingly enough, the hoarder called Old Dog Haven to talk about each of the dogs we'd taken and all she said about Aaron was that there seemed to be "something wrong with his rear end." I should also say here that the dogs that came from this particular hoarder weren't tied up outside. All of them lived in the house. They were very well socialized and it seemed clear that on some level they were loved and cared about. Cared about, but not cared for. Somehow there was a kind of disconnect when it came to knowing that something was wrong and still not providing any kind of medical care for any of the dogs.

Since Aaron's tumor could not be removed, Linda provided pain medication and anything else he needed—including a much needed trip to the groomers—to keep him comfortable and give him a reasonably good quality of life until the pain became too difficult to manage.

Aaron settled into his new home instantly and bonded immediately with Linda, as she did with him.

Linda remembers that one of Aaron's favorite things to do was to climb into a box that the cats used to play hide and seek. He thought the box was a great place to take a short nap.

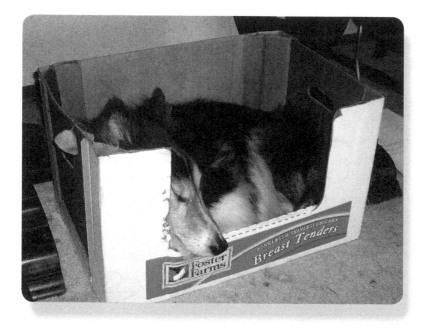

"He was a very gentle and well behaved dog," Linda says. "He just wanted to be near me and petted often. He seemed to be starving for attention as much as his body was starving for nutrients."

After only one week with Linda, Aaron's pain couldn't be controlled any longer so Linda took the day off work and spent the day with Aaron. When it was time for him to leave his body, she held him in her arms as he went Home very quietly without fear or discomfort.

"He will be missed for all of my life."

I've included Aaron's story in this book not only to illustrate the devastating effects hoarding has on animals, but also to make a point about an important aspect of what we do at Old Dog Haven. Well over 90% of the senior dogs that come to us are permanent Final Refuge dogs, not considered adoptable. Some are able stay a few days, weeks, or months, and some even live for three or four years. Sometimes good vet care and nursing can give the dog more time, but often we can only offer comfort and love. On occasion, as with a dog that lived with me for only six hours, our role is not long-term rehabilitation, but to be the one person in that dog's life who understands that the dog is suffering and is willing to release him from a body that has failed him. Hospice care is the most important thing we do. No old dog should have to die with strangers, terrified and confused in a concrete kennel. That's what would have happened to Aaron if Old Dog Haven hadn't agreed to take him.

Aaron was only with Linda for one week, and yet she says she will miss him for all of her life. If Aaron had that kind of impact on a woman who only knew him for seven days, think about how Aaron must have felt about her. Dogs live in the moment; it didn't matter to Aaron that he was only with Linda for a short time. What mattered to him was that every moment he was with Linda he felt loved, safe, and valued.

That's why we do this work.

MILLIE

"They just need to be happy and they forget about all the rest."

Judith and Lee have lived with many dogs at Home Base over the years. When I asked them to talk about those dogs that were especially helpful in teaching them a variety of important lessons that would prove useful as they continued to care for old dogs, they both named Millie immediately.

Millie came to Judith and Lee in March 2005 after Judith bailed her out of the shelter. Her age was listed as fourteen, although Judith thought she was "ancient." She appeared to be blind and deaf.

What Millie had to teach Judith and Lee became evident the moment she walked in the door. Lee led her around the house on a leash just once, and that was all it took for Millie to learn her way around. From that moment on Millie never bumped into anything or ran into any of the other dogs. Millie was blind and deaf but she wasn't disabled.

In spite of her being able to find her way around the house, Millie was stressed. She walked in circles when she was outside, and when she was in the house she paced. Judith spent the first two nights with her on the couch so she wouldn't continue to pace through the night.

Judith started Millie on medication to calm her and soon the pacing went away. This change in behavior is a valuable lesson to people who don't understand that the initial behavior a dog exhibits when coming into a new home, especially a dog coming from a shelter, doesn't always continue and can often be handled with medication, time, love, and the absence of stress.

As time passed, Millie settled in and felt secure. She loved being outside in the pasture and would dance in what Judith called "silly puppy circles" out in the field.

Millie lived with Judith and Lee for over a year before her old body finally failed her. Judith says, "She spent eighteen months with us, long after she should have faded away, and showed us how a very handicapped creature could cope with life. We loved her a great deal."

Judith with Millie

GRETCHEN

Lost and Found

In 2011, the day before Thanksgiving, a dog was found wandering on the Tulalip Reservation. An unknown man took the dog to his home where he fed her some beef stew. The man then called the police, who took the dog to the Everett Animal Shelter.

The intake report for the stray dog reads like an entry in a journal from Dachau; words like "unable to stand, severely matted, coated with feces and urine, severely dehydrated, sunken eyes, emaciated, swelling, infection, severe periodontal disease" are all found in the report along with one final entry: "find rescue."

After the required hold period had expired and no one had come to claim the dog, the shelter called Old Dog Haven and asked if we would take the dog. Enter long-time foster, Barb Bauer, who will tell you about her new friend, Gretchen:

"Judith contacted me to see if I might want to take on a very tough case. Judith said the dog may not survive and if she did it would be a long road ahead. She gave me every outlet to say no, but I needed a project. Our four Old Dog Haven dogs were doing wonderfully and were so easy to care for that I quickly said yes.

"When I arrived at the shelter, the staff was clearly thrilled and grateful that this dog was going to Old Dog Haven. When they brought her out to me she looked like the skeleton of Lassie. There was a thin, stained Seattle Mariners T-shirt on her (I am sure the best the shelter had to offer) and she looked bewildered. I fought down a rising lump in my throat when I saw the bones poking out everywhere and the sunken eyes. She dutifully followed me to the car and stood while I easily lifted her 23-pound body into the back seat. The stench coming from her was choking me, and I felt again like crying for her. I spoke quietly to her on the ride to her new home, not knowing if she could even hear, trying to reassure her that all would be okay now. This was Nov 28th and it was cold, so I stopped at Pet Pros and purchased a fleece lined large coat and wrapped it over her. The coat should have been too small for a dog of her stature, but it hung awkwardly over her bones.

"Dr. O'Connor of Frontier Village Veterinary Clinic performed the initial exam. He said little during that time. Blood was drawn and lateral X-rays taken. A badly infected toe was a concern so antibiotics were immediately prescribed. I kept remarking on what a sweet girl she was, and Dr. O'Connor just said, 'What choice does she have? This is one very sick dog.'

"Once home, the introduction to the pack was effortless. They knew immediately that this new one was not a threat and they gave her a wide berth. I had two large dog beds available to her and encouraged her to rest after feeding her a small amount of canned food. There was a lot of resting the first few weeks.

"Blood work results were ominous. She had managed to maintain proper kidney function, which was good news considering the extreme starvation, but her red blood count was seriously low. Was there a bleeding tumor? Cancer? A more intense X-ray was recommended to search for a possible mass. Gretchen had to lie on her back for this one, and it was terribly difficult because her spine had no cushion whatsoever. She complied and did not fight the techs who had the unpleasant task of restraining her. Her back became bruised because of the position she needed to assume for the X-ray, but thankfully no mass was found.

"So, we just waited and hoped the nutritious food and time would put her right. The first few days, I found Gretchen to be willing to do anything I might ask of her. Of course, she gobbled her food down and wanted more, but I knew I had to introduce larger portions and more caloric food slowly and she was gracious about it all. She asked to be let out when needed, but hesitated at the door because she was afraid she would not be let back in. So we all went out together. Weeks went by and more blood work showed no improvement. She was affectionate toward my husband, Bob, and I, but reserved. Some weight was gained and a little more interest in daily life was shown. I found Gretchen's hearing was perfect and her eyesight was good. She was very obedient, coming when called and showing no food aggression despite all she had been denied.

"Constantly I turned over possible scenarios in my mind: 'Had someone deliberately starved her? Had she been lost for a very long time? Did she live with someone who suffered from dementia?'

"Clearly she was housebroken and showed no fear of humans, but was extremely comfortable and familiar with the outdoors. My guess is that she spent many years outside left to her own devices. I sponge bathed her because the weather was cold and she was frail. The dandruff and scales slowly lessened and the lingering animal scat stench finally disappeared.

"By January, we were watching a more energetic and engaged dog emerge and new blood work showed some improvement! She was still not well enough to have a dental or to undergo surgery to have her troublesome toe removed, but Gretchen was now wanting to play with her pack mates and beginning to let her lovely personality shine. She began to be impish, harmlessly taking items from purses or wastebaskets and bringing them to us. Her tail wagged more and more. She began to tree squirrels and explore her two acres with gusto. Car rides were a good thing now! Her large coat no longer hung on her but looked the perfect fit. A soft, full coat was growing nicely with beautiful markings. She had gained eight pounds! She began to talk. A low grumbly moan sound meant she was happy. I would hear this sound and look to see what she was up to. Usually she had collapsed on her bed and was rolling around happily.

"By early March, her blood work was normal! Bob, I, Judith and the vet clinic staff (Gretchen had won over the staff at the clinic very early in her battle to get well) let out a collective WHOO HOO! Her toe ceased to be a problem and she had twelve teeth removed. I know she felt wonderful.

"Gretchen demands her fair share of love and affection in a very sweet way and barks in excitement for meals (will stop immediately if shushed). She is now actively THINKING she is treeing squirrels, but the squirrels leap from tree to tree to escape. Gretchen is oblivious to this trickery and sits or lies beneath the tree waiting and waiting. This morning I felt a light touch on my head as I was still sleeping. I opened my eyes to see Gretchen's nose lightly poking me as she let out her low, grumbly happy moan. Breakfast time."

Gretchen lived happily with Barb and Bob for nearly two years—a very long time for a dog that wasn't expected to survive a week—before her body failed her. While she was with them, Barb and Bob celebrated Gretchen every day, and even now they remember her with love and thanks for all she taught them.

PENNY

"A Perfect Best Friend"

The welfare of a dog in the care of someone who suffers from Alzheimer's disease is often at risk unless someone intervenes and assumes responsibility for the dog. Alzheimer's is so difficult and frustrating for not only the person dealing with the illness, but family members as well, that the dog often gets lost in the shuffle.

In 2005, the early days of Old Dog Haven, Judith was contacted by the grandchildren of a woman who was about to leave her own home and enter a special care facility for people with Alzheimer's disease. Judith and Lee agreed to take Penny the dog and she came to live with them at Home Base.

When Penny arrived, Judith was "... horrified at her condition. She'd itched herself so badly that much of her coat was gone and what could be seen was blackened 'elephant' skin. A huge hematoma in one ear had folded it down, and the skin was pulled down over her eye. There was a big swatch of black scarring from her ear down over her eye and down her cheek."

The grandchildren explained that Grandma just sat on the couch with Penny feeding her hot dogs. They knew the dog had fleas and allergies, but Grandma didn't want to leave the house to take the dog to the vet. Why they couldn't have taken Penny for treatment themselves, or applied flea treatment monthly, or given her anti-itch medicines they couldn't say. They were embarrassed, but not enough to have taken action.

Judith says that "Penny was one of the nicest, most lady-like dogs I've ever known, so we threw ourselves into fixing up the mess. The vet started her on medication to control the itch and heal her skin and ear infections. Good diet, flea preventative, medicated baths, fresh air and exercise were the rest of it. Penny took some time to get over her grief at losing Grandma, but we got her physically fixed up and she began to think life was pretty good, so it was time to find her a home of her own."

Penny's picture and profile, describing her as "short, stout but very loving" were posted on the website, and Judith soon received an inquiry from Cheryl Fontaine, who said that she too was short, stout and very loving. Cheryl came to meet Penny and their new life together began in what Judith describes as a "wonderful match that made me extremely happy."

Penny was the first, but not the last Old Dog Haven dog to find her way to Cheryl.

"When she came to live with me, her fleas had been taken care of, and with the exception of some wicked arthritis in her back and some wacky legs, she was a healthy girl."

Cheryl describes Penny as a "serious dog. Judith, who has an uncanny ability to know where a dog will fit in, told me that all Penny needed was a person to take care of."

Penny did her job. Each day, she accompanied Cheryl to the mailbox, which is quite a distance from her front door. Cheryl says, "The first time she walked with me, I had her on leash and dropped it when I got about twenty feet from

the mailbox. I held up my hand and told her to 'stay.' She stayed, and she stayed every single time after that without having to be told, without being on leash. For four years we took that walk together every day. During her last year, the pain in her legs and hind end had progressed enough that the trip to the mailbox had to end, but she waited for me at the distance she could go."

Penny always made sure she could see Cheryl. If Cheryl was outside gardening in the front, Penny would be watching her from the deck. If Cheryl moved to the side of the house, Penny would be close by, keeping an eye on her. When Cheryl was in the house, Penny followed her everywhere.

"She protected me. That was her job. And I always felt safe. She was a no nonsense dog."

About a month before Penny died she had a small stroke from which she recovered in a day or so, but the vet told Cheryl that she needed to be prepared because more strokes would occur in time, and eventually there would be one from which there could be no recovery.

When Cheryl got up on the morning of August 6, 2010, Penny wasn't up and about, wagging her tail, waiting for breakfast. Instead, Penny was lying in her bed, not moving. Cheryl says, "I went ahead and fed the other animals, with her not moving on her bed and me knowing something was horribly wrong. She'd had another stroke during the night. She could not move or even stand. She was humiliated that she had wet her bed. That's okay. I have a lot of dog beds."

That night Cheryl slept beside Penny on the floor. "I'm so happy I did because it was her last night before crossing the Rainbow Bridge."

Time has passed since Penny left Cheryl, but Cheryl remembers her with such love it could have been yesterday that Penny went on to her next expression of spirit. The two "short, stout and very loving" friends spent four years together.

Cheryl says that Penny was "a perfect best friend. She was brilliant, she was loyal, and she never stopped loving or being totally devoted. She just did her job and did it very well. I learned from her and am trying every day to measure up."

BRIDGETTE

"… the elder stateswoman of the family."

Have you ever wondered what happens to show dogs that are no longer able to compete in the ring? I'm not an expert on the subject because I haven't spent much time around show dogs, but I do know that many show dogs retire gracefully by spending their golden months or years strutting their stuff in dog parks somewhere and practicing the art of being couch potatoes in the comfort of their own homes, surrounded by family who love them. But not all former show dogs, especially the older dogs, live out their lives with the people who valued them when they were able to compete. They become expendable and are often abandoned when they've outlived their usefulness. Just like the dog you're about to meet.

Bridgette, a beautiful long-haired standard Dachshund, was brought to the vet by her person to be euthanized. The vet was told that Bridgette was "old," could no longer compete on the show circuit and needed to be released from her body. What the vet saw was a 14-year-old dog that was still reasonably healthy except for a bit of incontinence, typical Dachshund back issues, and some dementia. Bridgette's eyes were bright, she wagged her tail, and she was cheery and friendly. She wasn't done yet.

The vet refused to euthanize Bridgette and called Old Dog Haven. He explained the situation to Judith, who agreed to take Bridgette immediately and place her in a temporary foster home until she could find a permanent home for her. Fortunately, we have several foster families who are willing to take a dog immediately, and in this case, long-time foster mom Bernadette Huard came to the rescue, picked Bridgette up from the vet office and took her home with her until Judith could find a permanent Final Refuge home for her.

Shortly after Bridgette went to Bernadette's home, Judith received an email from Noel Kjosness, a woman who had seen Old Dog Haven's website and was interested in being an Old Dog Haven foster parent. Noel filled out the foster application and it wasn't long before Judith contacted her about Bridgette. Bridgette wasn't really happy being around all of Bernadette's other dogs, so the quiet home that Noel could offer her seemed perfect. It was perfect.

Noel met Bernadette and Bridgette in one of our famous "between-two-cities parking lots" south of Seattle one afternoon. Noel remembers seeing Bridgette get out of the car and thinking that she was "the longest dog I'd ever seen. She just kept coming."

Once Noel and Bridgette arrived home, Noel's other dogs, Sweet Pea, Coco Pup, and Sam—all rescues—accepted Bridgette immediately, and Noel could see that Bridgette was relieved to be in a quiet place with just three other dogs that were very respectful of her age and her need to be acknowledged as the elder stateswoman of the family.

Noel hadn't spent much time around older dogs, so living with Bridgette was a constant learning experience for her. When she and Bridgette would go for an evening walk in the neighborhood, Noel usually ended up carrying Bridgette at least part way home because when Bridgette got tired, she'd just stop, sit down, and wait for Noel to pick her up and carry her the rest of the way home. Noel is quite sure that the being carried part of the walk was what Bridgette liked most. Bridgette also liked meeting other dogs and having people stop and talk with her. Noel remembers that "she walked with her tail up over her back in true show dog style." Then, there was the matter of fitting through the doggie door. Bridgette, by now called "Miss B" by Noel, would get the front part of her body through the door and then get stuck and wait for

Noel to help her. So much for using the doggie door during the day while Noel was at work. Always willing to accommodate, Noel left the back door open slightly so that Bridgette could get out into the fenced yard during the day. Dealing with incontinence was also a new experience for Noel, but in true dog lover fashion she just shrugged and said, "I washed lots of throw rugs and then bought new ones when the old ones were too thin to use any longer." As time passed, Miss B also became a bit foggy because of the dementia that was lurking in the background, but Noel, once again, was there to help her make sense of whatever was going on and to reassure her that she was safe and well loved.

Regular grooming was no big deal for Bridgette because she was used to being fussed over and she handled trips to the groomer very well. She especially enjoyed having Noel and people they met on their walk tell her how beautiful she was.

Bridgette trusted Noel to keep her safe, comfortable and happy. She loved her lady and Noel says, "She wanted to be near me, but not necessarily held, unless we were coming home from a walk."

Bridgette lived happily with Noel and her little pack for fifteen months before she finally told Noel it was time for her to leave. She wasn't comfortable in her body any longer and the dementia was causing her to become uneasy. An aside here about dementia: People often overlook the devastating effects of dementia on dogs. I do understand that it's easier to know when to let a dog go if there are serious physical issues, but it's also important to acknowledge the mental and emotional issues as well as the physical problems and pay close attention to how a dog is responding to dementia. Some  dogs seem to handle it fairly well and aren't bothered particularly until the dementia becomes quite severe, but others, like Bridgette, become fearful and it isn't in their best interests to ask them to continue living with a mind that's failing them.

Noel didn't have any experience in releasing a dog from her body, but her connection with Miss B was so strong and clear that eventually she knew it was time. The night before Noel sent Miss B on her way, she talked with the other dogs about what was about to happen and before everyone went to bed, Sam, Coco Pup and Sweet Pea all made a deliberate point of stopping in front of Miss B as she was resting in her bed and saying good-bye to her. That night Miss B slept quietly because she knew it wouldn't be long before her lady would send her on her way.

The next day Noel came home from work early, fed Miss B her favorite dinner, went for a walk on the beach with her, and then brought her to the vet for her final visit. As she held Miss B, Noel whispered to her, "Show me where you're going." When Miss B left her body Noel saw a young and healthy dog running in a meadow, chasing butterflies. How cool is that?

Noel's experience with Miss B was so positive she's fostered fourteen dogs for Old Dog Haven since then and currently lives with three Old Dog Haven Final Refuge dogs and one puppy mill rescue dog. Noel says, "There's a huge value in old dogs; they're grateful for everything you do for them, and they give back without reservation. I'm very grateful to Old Dog Haven for making it possible for older dogs to have a second chance at happiness, and I love being a part of that experience."

TANNER

A Grand Old Man

On a cold winter day in January 2008 Tanner entered the lives of Judith and Lee. Tanner was turned in as a "stray" to a large shelter where he was put up for adoption with an estimated age of eight—a frequent "mistake" made by shelters hoping to find homes for senior dogs. Actually Tanner was probably closer to eighteen than eight; he was a very old guy.

When Tanner came to live with Judith and Lee at Home Base, he suffered from laryngeal paralysis (a common affliction of old labradors) and struggled to breathe. He could barely move his old joints and couldn't make it up the very shallow front steps without help. Judith and Lee didn't expect him to live through the week.

But … as is so often true of dogs that find themselves in a safe place with people who love them, Tanner became "younger" as time passed. He loved the pasture and was motivated to move around because he enjoyed spending time out there. Exercise, along with good food, supplements and medication allowed Tanner to enjoy a happy life with the Pipers for eight months.

Judith refers to Tanner as the "grand old man with a great smile. He had that labrador propeller tail to push him around the pasture. He was funny, he smiled a lot, and he had perfect house manners. From him we learned the protocol for old, overweight lame dogs, which has been put to frequent use for Old Dog Haven dogs. We have a written handout for other foster parents, in fact. After eight months of getting more mobile, more comfortable, and constantly wagging and smiling, he just couldn't do it anymore no matter how stubbornly he tried to hold on. We loved him a lot."

FRANCIS

He Saw With His Heart

Other rescue groups often contact Old Dog Haven if they have a senior dog in their care they don't think they will be able to place in an adoptive home. We're always happy to post dogs from other rescue groups on our website, and sometimes we have space available in one of our Final Refuge homes to take in a dog from another rescue organization.

We posted Francis as an "Urgent Need" on our website in August 2009, on behalf of a rescue group in the Puget Sound area. The story we were told was that Francis originally came from Post Falls, Idaho. He was found wandering in Post Falls, and since there isn't an Animal Control officer in Post Falls, the person who found him took him to the local police station.

We're not clear about how Francis came to the Puget Sound from Idaho, but the rescue group that had him didn't feel he was adoptable because not only was he an older dog, he didn't see or hear very well.

Tina Nabseth, our Transport/Placement Coordinator and one of our dedicated foster/Final Refuge parents, saw Francis' picture on our website, asked Judith about him, and when she found out that Judith had a home for Francis, Tina offered to pick him up from the rescue group representative who was fostering him. (Well, she actually offered the chauffer services of her husband, Rick, who is always ready and willing to help dogs.) It was decided that Tina and Rick would meet Francis' new family the next day on Whidbey Island where Old Dog Haven was having a picnic. That meeting never happened.

Once Rick arrived home with Francis, he and Tina realized that Francis really couldn't see anything at all and was quite deaf. Tina called Judith, who said that the home she had lined up for Francis really wouldn't be a good fit because his vision and hearing problems were more severe than she had been led to believe from the information she'd received. Francis was basically blind and deaf. (The information we receive from others about dogs we post on our website isn't always as accurate as it should be in order for us to make a good placement decision.)

Long story short, Tina and Rick offered to keep Francis with them and, as Tina says, "JACKPOT! We got the sweetest boy ever."

Francis, wherever he came from, probably lived most of his life outdoors. When he first came to the Nabseth home he wanted to be outside all the time. Tina isn't a believer in "outside dogs," so Francis' need to be outside was quite a challenge for her. Tina said, "Once winter came I was so afraid he'd freeze to death. He'd go to the back door constantly scratching to go out so I'd set the timer for 10-15 minutes and let him be outside. He loved the cold weather, but I'd bring him back in until the next time he went to the door. We played this game all winter long. I just wanted Francis to be comfortable inside and know that he was safe and loved."

One morning in January 2010, Tina saw that one of Francis' eyes was closed and he seemed to be in pain. She brought him to an eye specialist who told her that the pressure was very high in both eyes. A decision needed to be made: either remove the eyes, or release Francis from his body. Tina and Rick worried that Francis' heart might not be able to handle the surgery, but after much agonizing, they decided to go ahead with the surgery.

Francis did very well during surgery, and he recovered quickly. Tina says, "We were so happy for him, relieved for us and so very thankful to Old Dog Haven for giving him the chance to keep going, despite the cost. My friend Donna put it beautifully when she said, 'You see more with your heart than anything else,' and that is Francis. He just trusted everyone and maneuvered around here just fine. The surgery took him out of his misery and gave him more time here with us. Everywhere he went, people asked about his story. I was so proud to tell them about Old Dog Haven and the life they allowed him to have with us."

Eventually, Francis enjoyed being in the house more often. At night Tina would put him on the couch with her because he loved affection and being touched and she loved watching his little stub of a tail wag with joy as he shared a little special time with his "mom."

Francis had a way of touching people, and Tina and Rick provided plenty of opportunities for him to do that. He was a wonderful ambassador for Old Dog Haven as he attended many events, often riding in a fancy stroller that allowed him to just relax and not worry about navigating strange places.

For a dog that dealt with what most humans would call serious limitations, Francis was never afraid or shy around people. He trusted everyone. And, he would often come home smelling of perfume because so many women wanted to hug him. Judith says, "what a wonderful gift he was to all. He was such a star at the auction too, and he had more impact on the attendees than any of the other dogs. It had to have been sensory overload for him, but he handled it so well."

Ambassadors can often be very effective teachers, and my favorite story about Francis involves his experience with children. After Marjorie Butcher's 2nd grade class from John Stanford International School in Seattle met Francis

when he came to their classroom to visit, they decided to do a fundraiser for Old Dog Haven. The class purchased reusable, recycled shopping bags, decorated them and decided to have a "bag sale" in front of a grocery store one weekend.

A week before the sale Francis had a serious seizure. Tina was afraid that he might not be able to attend the sale. She was concerned about how the class would handle his absence, but Marjorie Butcher chose the information Tina gave her about Francis' health to serve as a "teachable moment" for her class so they would understand why Francis might not be able to attend.

But Francis **did** attend the bag sale, much to the delight of his new fan club. He was charming as always and his gentle ways had a particularly profound effect on one of the students. Before she met Francis, Jaya had been afraid of dogs but on that day she and Francis became friends.

Tina says, "Francis made many friends at the bag sale and so I had to email the teacher, Marjorie Butcher, and tell her about his passing. When Marjorie told the class about Francis, there were some tears, so she had her students think about how much joy Francis had in his final years and how much he'd enjoyed meeting the kids. Marjorie sent me her condolences and then forwarded this message from Jaya, which I will forever cherish."

Thank you Francis.

You changed my life. Before I met you I was super scared of dogs. I would run away and cry. When you kept sniffing me at the bag sale I decided dogs can be safe. I love you so much. Thank you for what you did for me. My family was even able to dog-sit our friend's dog for 3 days. Now I want a dog.

Love, Jaya 8 ½ years old.

Even with some slight damage from a possible stroke, high blood pressure and a bit of dementia, Francis was happy and comfortable for almost three years with Tina and Rick. In early Summer 2012, tumors developed in his spleen, and Tina and Rick knew that it was time to send Francis on to his next expression of spirit.

Living with dogs is always a learning experience, and when I asked Tina what she learned from Francis her answer was immediate: "What

Francis and Jaya

I've learned from Francis is to trust more. We've had other blind dogs here and they all were much more nervous about new people or animals, but Francis was not. He just rolled with everything and everyone. Francis was incredibly special, and we feel so very fortunate to have known and loved him."

Sometimes when you follow the yellow brick road there's more at the end than you could possibly imagine. Perhaps Francis knew all along that if you have hope and are willing to trust people, despite whatever you've experienced, it's all good.

SIDNEY

*"He was one of those dogs that made you feel like
you were the most important person in the world to him."*

Most of the dogs that come to us are in pretty bad shape on so many levels. They know no one wants them, so their emotional health is fragile at best. In many cases they've been isolated, for one reason or another, so their socialization skills are often underdeveloped as well. In addition, most dogs come to us in poor physical condition.

To say that Sidney was a mess when he was brought in as a stray isn't even close to describing what he looked like when he was admitted to the shelter. The shelter notified Judith about this "pathetic" chocolate lab and hoped Old Dog Haven could take him.

Judith immediately emailed Kelly Marlo, one of our long-time fosters, who's seen just about everything in terms of dogs with physical and emotional issues. Judith gave Kelly a detailed description of Sidney's physical problems and included pictures taken of Sidney when he was first brought to the shelter.

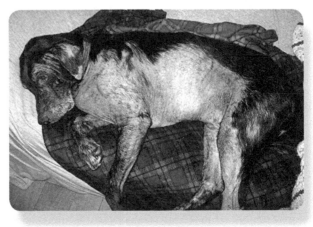

Judith was very up-front with Kelly about Sidney's condition and said she'd understand if Kelly felt that he might be too much for her in terms of rehabilitation.

Kelly, by her own admission, is "a big sucker for really pathetic, unadoptable or misfit creatures" so she wasn't put off at all and agreed to foster Sidney, hoping that he might be adoptable at some point in the future.

Kelly says, "After seeing the pictures, my heart absolutely broke for this dog. I agreed to take him immediately and picked him up at the shelter. He looked like a shell of a dog: he was missing most of his hair, his eyes were oozing, the skin on his face was chapped and red, there were open oozing hot spot wounds on all of his legs, and he had several very large tumors, which turned out to be lipomas, all over him. One was the size of a grapefruit!"

Kelly expected Sidney to be "a bit grumpy or depressed because he looked like he was in misery." Instead, Sidney wagged his tail, licked her and was excited to leave the shelter with his new friend. Sidney was happy, friendly, and affectionate from the moment he met Kelly.

Once they arrived at Kelly's house Sidney acted as if he had lived there his whole life. He hopped right up on the couch, and that's where he loved to be most of the time he stayed with Kelly.

Kelly brought Sidney to the vet immediately and then started him on medication and medicated shampoo baths. Because his skin condition was so severe Sidney needed baths every other day, but he never complained. He loved being with Kelly and knew she was trying to help him be well.

Kelly describes Sidney as "the most gentle, sweet natured dog I have ever met. He has the greatest personality and nothing bothers him. Despite all the neglect he has suffered, he loves people and trusts everybody. He is one of those unforgettable dogs. I don't think I have ever met a sweeter dog than Sid. He taught me how resilient and forgiving dogs can be. Even though he looked awful on the outside and no one had bothered to get him the medical care he needed prior to being taken in by Old Dog Haven, he would do anything to make me happy and was always grateful for what he was getting."

After two months of shampooing him every other day, high quality food, supplements and some serious TLC, Sidney was finally healthy enough to have surgery to remove the large growths on his body. Kelly then had to face the fact that Sid was looking much better and was very adoptable.

This realization—that a dog you have nurtured is finally ready to be adopted—is often a bittersweet moment for foster parents. Kelly had grown so attached to Sidney that a part of her selfishly wanted him to be unadoptable. But she also knew that Sidney needed his own home and shouldn't have to share affection with many other foster dogs.

Enter Janine Henkel.

In January 2011, Janine's beloved 14-year-old Husky, Koty, suddenly became ill and Janine needed to release him from his body. Janine says, "Koty's absence left such a hole in my heart that I didn't think anything would ever fill it. I have adopted three dogs from Old Dog Haven so far, the latest member being my 16-year-old lab mix "Zeus" that I got when he was only twelve. We would always joke about how Zeus and Koty acted like puppies all the time, whether it was on walks or in the house, to the point where they needed 'time outs' when they got out of hand. In the days that passed after Koty's death, Zeus became lethargic. He wasn't as energetic around the house and sort of just limped along on our walks. So I made the call to Judith and told her I needed a new oldie for our home."

Judith told Janine about Sidney and a meeting with Kelly and Sidney was arranged. Janine recalls, "Something about Sidney immediately made us realize he was our new family member. Maybe it was his peaceful brown eyes. You could tell he hid so much pain from his past life. Kelly could not say enough wonderful things about him. He wasn't beautiful, but he was so sweet and kind.

"We scooped him up and took him home. For a few days Sid kept to himself like a polite houseguest. He went for walks, slept, ate, but otherwise just kept to himself on his dog bed. He still had issues with hotspots, was missing fur on his chest and needed to gain about fifteen pounds. His coat was dull, his ears had some sort of fungus growing inside and he smelled terrible after multiple baths. Kelly had given us medication and instructions for poor Sid, but I decided to take him to my vet just to be sure."

Janine says that her vet and the entire staff immediately fell in love with Sid. They doted on him for about thirty minutes, and then he got a complete checkup. Janine left with more medications for Sid. After about four weeks with Janine, Sid's energy exploded, the funky smell went away, his coat was shiny, and he gained about fifteen pounds. He became excited and happy all the time. Sid's renewed youth even affected Zeus, who suddenly became his old, active self again.

Janine says, "I can say with all my heart that Sid is the nicest, sweetest dog I have ever known. He has turned into a healthy, robust, 85-pound chocolate lab that is full of life!

"When I see his 'before' pictures, I can't even believe it's him. He is such a character and makes us laugh several times a day. He is a great combination of perfect family dog (my old foster cats can walk all over him) and the guardian of the house. Everyone who meets Sid falls for his sweet brown eyes immediately. I actually had a shop owner beg me to let her have him!

"My only regret in getting Sid is that I wish he had come to me years earlier. Nevertheless, I know that with love and a healthy environment, Sid will fill our family with lots of laughs and love for years. Sid is the fourth dog I have adopted from Old Dog Haven and the fifth 'oldie' that I've ever had. All of them lived long, healthy lives. They were all perfect."

I wish I could end this chapter with the above paragraph, but I need to tell the whole story. In November 2011, Janine contacted Kelly to let her know that Sid was having trouble getting around on their hardwood floors and up their front stairs. Kelly was planning to dog sit for Janine around Thanksgiving and she had told Janine she would always take Sid back into her care if he was having a tough time getting around. So, Sid went back to Kelly. The rest of the story you need to hear from her:

"I felt like he was probably just meant to be with me, and so we kept him as a Final Refuge dog. I didn't know how true that would be, since I assumed he would be with me for a while. When he came back, it was like he had never left. He resumed his place right next to my side of the bed and was my little Velcro baby. He was one of those dogs that made you feel like you were the most important person in the world to him. He didn't have ulterior motives, wasn't looking for a treat or to be rubbed, although he would gladly take any of the above. He just wanted to spend time with me. We would spend our nights cuddled up on the couch, his head on my lap and the warm electric blanket he loved on top of him. He would do anything just to get up on the couch with me and just had to be as close as possible! I have never met a dog so kind, so friendly and so gentle. He never got into any trouble, never growled and always listened. He loved every person he met, every dog he encountered and was just so happy and grateful to have a safe home.

"About two months ago, he wouldn't eat, which is very unlike him. Judith recommended we get him in for some lab work and X-rays, which showed a huge grapefruit sized tumor in his abdomen. Surgery didn't sound like a good option for him since he didn't have a great immune system and his neurological problems started getting more evident. We decided we would just spoil him and enjoy the days we had left together. We spent his last days eating a bit too much, snoozing and lying out in the sun. Last Friday I knew our time was up and we had to release him from his failing body.

"I am so grateful to all of you at Old Dog Haven for rescuing a dog like Sid and giving him the life he truly deserved. I will cherish all the great memories I had with him. He passed away knowing he was truly loved."

I never had the pleasure of meeting Sid, but as I read what Janine and Kelly had to say about him it's very clear that he brought out the best in everyone who loved him. In his obituary, posted on our website, Judith described him as "a very special dog with a wonderful soul." She certainly got that right.

QUEENIE

"She was The Queen ... a gracious spirit"

Have you thought about what will happen to your animals if you are no longer able to care for them? In the Supplementary Reading section at the end of this book I offer some thoughts on what you need to think about, as well as a plan to put in place. The bottom line is simple: **plan ahead**.

People often make assumptions about family and friends being willing to take their animals if they're unable to care for them, but those assumptions don't always prove true, as was the case for the dog in this story.

Queenie's human friend died suddenly in an automobile accident, and Queenie was brought to the animal shelter because there was no one willing or able to care for her. An old dog suddenly loses her best friend, isn't comforted by anyone she knows, and she ends up in a cage.

As is true of so many of the stories in this book, Old Dog Haven was called by the shelter and Judith and Lee took Queenie into their own home because there were no other foster homes available at the time.

I should mention that when Queenie was brought to the shelter, she came with the name her human friend had chosen for her. Queenie isn't a name Judith and Lee would typically choose for a dog, but they honored the memory of Queenie's human friend and didn't change Queenie's name. As time passed, it became very clear that it was a perfect name for her because, as Judith says, "She just WAS a Queenie."

Queenie—a 13-year-old oversized black lab mix—was actually healthy when she came to Home Base. Someone had taken very good care of her. She passed her initial vet exam with flying colors. At 113 pounds, she was carrying a bit too much weight, but that was easily taken care of during the four years she spent with Judith and Lee. Yes, I said four years. Queenie lived to be seventeen and during those four years she never had anything wrong with her except for once needing a root canal. Judith says, "She never looked a day over eight years old, until the last year. She never even needed joint supplements or any kind of medication."

Queenie was the Queen … the ultimate alpha dog. All of the other dogs knew Queenie was the boss and any of them that even had tentative ideas about becoming the pack leader were immediately convinced to think otherwise by Queenie. It wasn't that she behaved aggressively toward the other dogs; she just was such a considerable presence that none of the dogs, except Ellie, ever questioned her authority.

I remember coming to see Judith and Lee one summer day. As soon as I arrived at the gate the dogs outside came toward the gate to greet me. It was like the parting of the Red Sea as Queenie came toward the gate. The other dogs moved out of her way so she could be the first to greet me. She actually liked the other dogs and they liked her. They just didn't mess with her because she had this alpha aura about her that told everyone she was in charge.

As is true of all the dogs at Home Base that have reasonable mobility, Queenie loved the walks at the tree farm. Naturally, she led the pack, and

Judith remembers that she "galloped like a Budweiser Clydesdale." I never saw Queenie gallop at the tree farm, but I did see her lope around the pasture and the image of a Clydesdale is perfect.

As pack leader, Queenie took her duties very seriously even when it came to overseeing her property. Every night, without exception, she became the wild-life warden as she walked the perimeter of the property. She didn't bark. She didn't make a fuss. She just made her presence known. She could easily have been carrying a sign that said, "Lions and tigers beware! Queenie is on patrol."

Lee remembers that Queenie was "the best ball player we've ever had here. She loved to play ball, and she even brought it back!"

Queenie never thought of herself as an old lady. Even during her last year with Judith and Lee she aged gracefully and was, according to Judith, "a class act that old lady. What a kick she was!"

But, regardless of how young she felt, Queenie's body aged and finally gave out on her. Her reign finally ended and, as Judith says, "our tough old lady left us at age seventeen with her gracious spirit still intact. She has left a large hole, but a lot of happy memories."

She **was** a gracious spirit. I'm very happy I knew her.

PANCAKE

If ever a dog needed to know he was loved, it was Pancake.

I need to warn you that it will be difficult for you to read this story. Also, some of the photographs are very graphic and are the worst examples of severe neglect that I've ever seen. I actually did think about not including Pancake's story because it's so disturbing, but I decided that the memory of this brave little dog needed to be honored, and telling his story is a way to do that. I also wanted to acknowledge the efforts of the Whatcom Humane Society because they saved his life and made it possible for him to have an opportunity to be loved and nurtured by two of Old Dog Haven's Final Refuge moms.

One a hot day in July 2009, an out-of-state salesman found what appeared to be a dog lying on top of a black garbage bag on the porch of a house in Bellingham.

The salesman thought the dog was dead, but when he touched him he realized that he was still breathing. The salesman knocked on the door, but when no one answered he went to the house next door. The neighbor said he would immediately call the Whatcom Humane Society about the dog.

Pancake when found.

Paul Evans was the responding Animal Control Officer. Officer Evans' report contains the following statements: "I responded to that location and found a small-to-medium sized dog covered in matted fur on the porch near the main door to the residence. The dog was whimpering and could not move. Every time the dog tried to shake its head it couldn't because the mats on its ears were too heavy. I knocked on the door, but there was no answer. The dog was in such poor condition I believed it would have suffered more and possibly died being left there. I then took the dog to Maplewood Animal Hospital."

When Officer Evans arrived at Maplewood, he was joined by other Animal Control officers as well as a Whatcom County Deputy who had been monitoring Officer Evans' call and heard him say that he was transporting a dog whose condition was "the worst I've ever seen."

Excerpts from the initial examination by the Animal Control officers include the following statements: "appeared to be a pile of fur" … "indistinct appendages" … "a very strong odor of ammonia and animal stench" … "the dog was motionless and appeared immobile."

The dog was carried into the animal hospital on a stretcher and placed on the examination table where he was seen by Dr. Christine Monroe, DVM. Officer Evans' report states that "the staff that was present showed a visibly emotional response to the dog's appearance." Dr. Monroe examined the dog, determined that he was alive and stated that she wanted to try to save him. Dr.

Monroe then had her staff begin the process of removing the matted fur from the dog. This procedure took approximately three hours and was documented with narrative and photographs taken by a Whatcom County deputy.

The Case View Report includes the following observations by the deputy present at the three hour procedure: "Most notable was the overall condition presented by the dog, evidenced by the extreme matting and odor. The dog moved very little, but remained in the splayed posture first observed. The dog's eyes were barely visible and apparently not functioning. There was a significant bare area along the forward half of the dog's backbone, which revealed a very skinny spine. The ears were notable as they laid away from the dog's head and emphasized its very thin neck. The dog's legs were indistinct due to the heavily matted fur. As the vet tech removed the fur, a beetle fell off the dog's body. When the hair was clipped from the skull, the left side of the dog's head appeared very red and bumpy. At one point in this stage, maggots were discovered in and around the dog's left eye, ear opening and then inside the ear canal. A sample of the maggots was saved for evidence. Both eyes looked to be blind. The clipping process moved to the body, then to the legs, tail and returned to the head. When the paws were uncovered, the pads appeared to be in poor shape. Their appearance was dry, rotted, cracked and looked as if they were flaking or cracking away on their surface. The claws were extremely long, one on each front foot being about as long as two to three U.S. quarter coins. They were oddly curved and misshapen. The longest two were collected as evidence. The dog has several burns on its body caused by urine, according to the vet staff. There was one significant lesion on the dog's right front leg.

"When the dog was completely clipped it looked very skinny and malnourished.

"The dog did exhibit more movement and signs of life after its fur was removed. The dog then was washed and treated with a skin lotion. It should be noted that maggots continued to emerge from the dog's left ear even after the bathing. Both the dog and removed fur were weighed by the vet staff and compared to the initial weighing. I noted the voiced weight readings as: before: 18.5 pounds, after: 13.65 pounds, removed fur: 4.95 pounds."

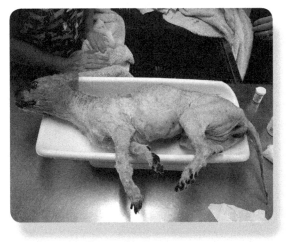

Even though Dr. Monroe's evaluation of the dog echoes some of the observations made by the deputy, I include her notes here in their entirety to offer medical validation of the dog's condition: "Whatcom County Animal Control presented canine patient on stretcher. Patient was splayed/recumbent on presentation. Patient was a male neutered canine unrecognizable breed. Weight approx. 18.5#.

"Patient had severe generalized hair matting to the extent I could not even recognize patient as a dog until it shook its head. The patient was weak and unable to move due to the inhibition of movement due to the extent of the matting and the weight of the mats. Mats covered entire canine. Ears, body, face, back, tail, and legs/paws could not be recognized due to mats which were at least 6cm thick. I could visualize overgrown toenails sticking out of the mats. Mats were urine and feces soaked. The matting around the face, ears, and head contained a large volume of fly eggs and maggots. The right eye is enlarged and has chronic granulation tissue over entire cornea with a central divot lesion. The left eye has micro ophthalmia and the cornea is pigmented. Both eyes contained maggots under both upper and lower lids. Oral exam revealed periodontal disease.

"The patient was administered subcutaneous fluids, penicillin, analgesia, and an anesthetic. The patient was completely shaved—groom time 3 hours. 4.95# of mats were collected. Post shaving revealed the patient had severe moist dermatitis/tissue scald/erythema of the face, neck, ears, and ventrum with other multifocal areas over body and legs. The right ear canal was filled with maggots and other superficial areas on the head and neck contained maggots. The right elbow and both hocks have ulcerative lesions secondary to the matting. The scrotal area has an approx. 6cm x 2cm adherent necrotic area of skin. Both front P2 claws were 6cm in length and several of the rear claws were grown in 'coils.' Patient is extremely thin. The body score is 1/5 (3 is optimum and 5 is obese). Approx. 6-7% dehydration noted.

"Patient was bathed in medicated shampoo and creme rinse and the ears and eyes were flushed to remove the maggots. Anti-inflammatory medication was administered. The patient was placed on heat to recover. The patient will be placed on appropriate medications.

"This canine patient is a case of extremely severe neglect. I estimate the severe hair/urine/feces matting has been occurring over approx. a year's time and the maggot infestation occurring over the past week due to the extreme temperatures and humidity."

Dr. Monroe, who has practiced veterinary medicine since 1993, was later quoted in the *Bellingham Herald* as stating, "This was by far the worst case of cruelty and neglect I've ever seen."

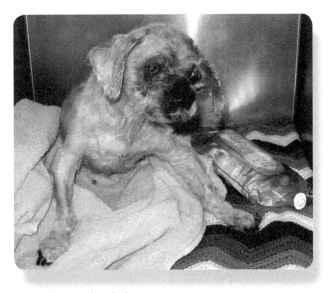

Pancake at the shelter

If you're still with me, we can now move on to the healing part of this story. The dog, now named Pancake by shelter staff, remained in the custody of Whatcom Humane Society for two months while the legal aspects of his case were handled and resolved. During his stay at the Whatcom Humane Society Shelter Pancake was **very** well cared for by staff, and in September 2009 he was officially transferred to Old Dog Haven.

Judith asked Final Refuge moms Darci Bonsen and Amy Devon if they would be willing to care for Pancake for the rest of his life. Darci and Amy agreed immediately, with the understanding that this little dog had been through so much that he might not be able to stay in his body for a long time. Darci and Amy understand that dogs live in the moment, and they were determined to fill Pancake's every remaining moment on this earth with love, comfort, and security.

There was no dramatic recovery for Pancake, but Darci and Amy loved the small victories they saw each day. Darci says, "He came to us damaged, depressed and scared, but he did come around. He was afraid to move at first so housebreaking took some time. He wandered the house, and loved to lie in the sunshine. He would move from place to place, following the warmth. His favorite snack was cheese, and he would let us know when he was hungry; he would walk over to the pantry door and just stand there until he was fed."

Pancake's eyes began to really bother him and it was decided that the eyes needed to be removed since they weren't functioning at all and were causing such discomfort. Darci says, "When he recovered from the surgery he seemed better for a while. He loved the gentle touch of a hand, and would even seek it out."

Pancake at home with Darci and Amy

Unfortunately, the years of neglect finally caught up with Pancake. After a little over two months with Darci and Amy they decided that "his quality of life was not what we wanted for him and it was time to let him go over the Rainbow Bridge. It was a very sad day for us. We know he was thankful to be here even for a short period of time. Pancake did not deserve the treatment he received, as no animal should. Having taken care of him was something that made us proud, even though the time was short. When he left us we felt good about his last months, knowing he is now playing happily over the Rainbow Bridge."

Pancake existed for seventeen years, but his life in this world actually began on July 31, 2009 when he was rescued by Officer Evans. It ended on November 24, 2009 when Darci and Amy released him from his damaged body.

On May 2, 2010 Old Dog Haven was presented with a Woof and Whisker Award from Whatcom Humane Society for our work with Pancake. This is the second award Old Dog Haven has received from WHS. We really appreciate their efforts to recognize those in the community who help homeless animals.

I know you've been waiting to read what legal action was taken with regard to Pancake, but I didn't want to interrupt my narrative of his story to relay the information contained in Pancake's case file. I'll summarize here: Since Officer Evans received no response when he knocked on the door of Pancake's house, before he removed Pancake from the premises he spoke with the neighbor who had called Whatcom Humane and was told that the owner's name was John. (fictitious name) After Officer Evans delivered Pancake to the veterinary hospital, he then went to John's place of business where he spoke with him at length. The conversation as related in the case report is convoluted and contradictory, but the bottom line is that John said that he and his wife, Mary (fictitious name) thought Pancake was dead so they put him on the porch because "he wasn't making any noise." When questioned about vet care or whether he and his wife had considered euthanasia for Pancake, John gave conflicting statements about any vet care and stated emphatically that they didn't believe in euthanasia and wanted the dog to die naturally. He also said that Pancake's name was Ralf, and that he was seventeen years old, and had lived with him and his wife (a nurse) for thirteen years.

The final disposition of the case, according to the Whatcom County Prosecutor's office was that John and Mary were each charged with one count of animal cruelty in the second degree, a gross misdemeanor. The case never went to trial. Charges against John were dropped and his wife pled guilty. Her sentence was jail converted to forty hours of community service, $502 restitution paid to Maplewood Animal Hospital, and a civil penalty of $1,000.00.

If ever a dog needed to know he was loved it was Pancake. Because of the efforts of the many people who intervened on Pancake's behalf, with proper medical attention his body healed as well as it could considering the damage that had been done over the years. He did experience kindness, compassion and love, if only for a short period of time.

ERNESTO

"He's not disabled. He's differently abled."

Parking lots in shopping malls and those located in front of large retail stores are convenient locations for people who don't want their dogs. Dogs are just dumped, with no thought for their safety or well-being. The thinking here is the same song you've heard before: let someone else assume responsibility.

In October 2010, a pug was found wandering around the parking lot of the Walmart in Shelton, Washington. The dog was taken to the city animal shelter. The dog was obviously older, so the Animal Control officer contacted one of our foster moms, Trisha Lovgren, who volunteers at the shelter, because she knew Trisha was also involved with Old Dog Haven. Trisha called Judith, and they decided that Trisha would take the pug and he would become an Old Dog Haven Final Refuge dog. Trisha says, "I wasn't immediately sure if he would stay with me or go into another Final Refuge home, as I was not entirely sure I was a good fit for him given his disabilities. But first he needed a name. I decided he was to be named Ernesto."

When Ernesto came to Trisha he hadn't been neutered. His eyes were red and inflamed. He appeared to be blind. He was deaf and had infections in both ears. He also had a crippled front right leg and shoulder.

Trisha took Ernesto to her veterinarian, Dr. Trish Roisum at Steamboat Animal Hospital, where he was given the usual workup. All of his lab work looked good so he was scheduled to be neutered and have his teeth cleaned. Dr. Roisum estimated Ernesto's age at twelve or thirteen.

After his initial vet appointment but before his surgery, Trisha decided to keep Ernesto permanently as a Final Refuge dog. She talked with Judith at length and says, "Judith assured me that caring for a blind and deaf dog was really not that much different than caring for a 'normal' dog. She said many dogs that were blind and deaf thrived, but there were some that did not handle those limitations very well. I could already tell Ernesto was one of those dogs that didn't let these problems slow him down. He had no fear. It was official … I had fallen in love with Ernesto!"

Ernesto and Trisha

Ernesto's neuter surgery went well, but it was decided that because his teeth were in very poor shape, he would need to see the oral surgeon in Shoreline. Dr.Roisum also took X-rays of Ernesto's crippled leg/shoulder. It was discovered that his shoulder had been broken at some point, and an attempt had been made to fix it by inserting a large metal rod, but the rod insertion hadn't been a successful solution. Trisha was very concerned about Ernesto being in pain, but Dr.Roisum assured her that the injury was not causing him any discomfort.

A month after his first surgery, Trisha drove Ernesto up to Shoreline to see Dr. DuPont at the Shoreline Veterinary Dental Clinic for his oral surgery/teeth cleaning. Dr. DuPont became an instant fan of this charming dog and always describes Ernesto as a "class act" every time he sees him.

Shortly after having his teeth fixed Ernesto was seen in Olympia by Dr. Cooley, a veterinary eye specialist. Dr. Cooley confirmed that Ernesto was indeed blind, and that his blindness was almost certainly a result of long-standing untreated dry eye. Dr. Cooley determined that Ernesto's eyes were not causing him any pain, but he would require eye drops every few hours for the rest of his life.

Ernesto and Dr. DuPont

In the first months after coming to live with Trisha Ernesto developed canine vestibular syndrome, which causes dogs to have a "drunk" type of motion because they've lost their sense of balance and orientation. Ernesto's symptoms came and went over a period of a few weeks, but he recovered fully even though he was left with a permanent slight head tilt, which is a common residual effect of vestibular syndrome. Trisha thinks that the head tilt "makes him just that much cuter."

Ernesto met the challenges of the various surgeries and medical treatment in true Ernesto style. Trisha says, "He amazed me. Here he was blind, deaf, and crippled. The shoulder injury left him with his shoulder fused in a bent position. This causes his paw on that leg to hit the ground knuckles first rather than paw first which has left him with a slightly deformed paw. But Ernesto is happy as can be and always seems to know who is in the room, when someone new enters the room, leaves the room, and so forth. Basically Ernesto always knows where the action is."

Trish says that Ernesto had only been living with her for a few days when he'd already memorized the layout of her large unfenced front yard. "You could set him 50' feet away in the corner of the property and sure enough he would find his way back to the driveway, up the sidewalk, and up the dog ramp, to scratch at the front door. Amazing! We moved to a new house four months after he came to live with me, and of course in a matter of days he had the new house and yard memorized."

Ernesto has been living with Trisha for about four years now and she says, "There's not a day goes by that I don't honor the fact that I am so lucky to have him in my life. I always think to myself when I'm going through one of life's struggles/mini-crises, 'If Ernesto can adapt then I can adapt.'

"Ernesto is a funny dog in more ways than one. He's funny looking (funny as in handsome), he's funny sounding (I swear he's half pig), and he's funny acting when he does his impression of a vacuum cleaner and slides across the carpet with his face turned sideways pressed against the floor. He pushes himself along the length of the room only changing direction when he finally bumps into something. You would think this would not be as funny after seeing him do it every single day, but it's just as funny as the first time I ever saw him do it.

"Ernesto is a brave, tough pup with a heart of gold. He loves to be snuggled, to have his belly rubbed, to sneak into my bed at night, and to steal his doggie brothers and sisters' food when I'm not looking. Ernesto is also quite the tug-of-war player and can growl during a match like no other."

Trisha often wonders what Ernesto's life was like before that day he was left in the Walmart parking lot. She wonders if anyone ever loved him. She wonders how many people he'd had in his life. She wonders what he was like when he could see, hear, and walk perfectly. Trisha has even had dreams "in which Ernesto is not blind, not deaf, and not crippled. In my dreams he can run and chase a ball. It brings tears to my eyes thinking about the dreams. But you know what? So what if he can't see, can't hear, and can't run. Ernesto is doing just fine and is enjoying his life despite his challenges. He's not disabled; he's differently abled."

I haven't ever met Ernesto, but every time I see his photo I can't help but smile. That lightness of spirit Trisha describes so well shines through his cute little body in every way possible.

RISHA

"… she knew she was loved and safe with us."

You probably can't imagine bringing your lifetime companion dog to a shelter, but for many people that seems to be their only option because they've made no other plans in case they are unable to care for the dog, for whatever reason. Or, as I've mentioned in the chapter about Queenie, people make assumptions about other family members being willing to care for their dog if they aren't able to do so, but those assumptions aren't always based in reality, and quite often the dog ends up at a shelter.

Risha was surrendered to a shelter by a retired couple who were dealing with their own medical issues and felt they could no longer care for the dog. Risha had lived with these people for many years, and she was most likely about twelve or thirteen when she came to the shelter. According to the information provided by her people, Risha had been kept in a separate room because they didn't want her to live in the family space. Later, after Old Dog Haven placed Risha in a home, it became clear that she had been most likely ignored and possibly abused in her previous home.

The vet records provided to the shelter indicated that Risha was current on her vaccinations, but no other care had been given to her in all of the years she had been with the people who had surrendered her. Risha weighed over thirty-four pounds when she was brought to the shelter, which is considered obese for a Cocker spaniel of her size. Her teeth were so rotten the smell pervaded the entire room, and she had many growths and tumors on several areas of her body. Her mobility was not good at all; she had a hard time getting up and had a profound limp.

Risha spent about a month at the shelter before Old Dog Haven was able to find a home for her, and shelter life was hard on her—as it is on all dogs that live in cages 24/7. Finally, a home became available with Mary and Dennis Staberg and Risha was removed from the shelter and brought directly to Mary and Dennis.

As is often the case, one of our transport volunteers picked Risha up from the shelter and met Mary and Dennis at a rest stop on I-5. Mary says, "I like to introduce new dogs to ours away from our home, so the rest stop was a good neutral ground. Risha growled at me, bit at my husband, and pretty much ignored our other dogs. An interesting start!"

Risha's new life with Mary, Dennis and their three other Cocker spaniels was a big change for Risha because not only had she been an only dog, she now found herself in a new home as well. Mary says Risha never really liked other dogs, but for the most part she "put up with ours, although sometimes out of the blue she would go after one of them. It was not just a warning; they would simply walk away from her when it happened but she would continue to go after them. But, all and all she adjusted quite well and she and I bonded quite quickly."

Risha's health needed attention as well as her emotional and social needs, so a long overdue trip to the vet involved removing **all** of her teeth as well as the growths and tumor. Incontinence issues were addressed with medication, and Mary started her on a diet and exercise program that resulted in Risha eventually reaching her goal weight of twenty-three pounds. She was able to keep up with the other dogs on walks and only a slight limp could be detected when she walked.

Risha was calm and quiet at home, but if someone said "walk" she would go into an excited dance—bumping into everyone and everything—so happy she just couldn't contain herself. Mary and Dennis drive to their walk destination and once in the car Risha would roll and roll in the crate with pure joy. Mary says, "I swear Risha must have had some hound in her breeding past because as soon as she was out of the car and back on the ground, her nose was to the ground to smell every last scent she could sniff. Even with the back and leg pain we now realize she must have always been in, she pulled the whole time she walked. There was no slow speed for Risha.

"When we would go for our walks she would bark at every dog and every person she would see. There are a few very nice dog people we stop and talk with most every day we walk, and I asked them for their help with Risha so she could hopefully become more trusting of people. I would bring dog treats for them to give her, and she did get better with those few people but was always on the defense. She would still lunge at any other people who might try to pet her and despite all my efforts that would never change."

As you probably know from your own experience, dogs love a routine and are comforted by the predictability of daily events. Risha's morning routine consisted of sitting outside the bedroom door while Dennis was still sleeping. This waiting time became so regular that Mary eventually put a little bed in front of the bedroom door so Risha could be comfortable while Mary took a shower and until Dennis joined her for breakfast. Risha was waiting for her dad—the man she tried to bite when she first met him.

For a while, Risha's outbursts toward the other dogs stopped, but then they started all over again and escalated in intensity. Mary reached a point where she didn't know what to do to help Risha. Mary felt that Risha's actions toward the other dogs indicated that she wanted to be an only dog and felt that perhaps Risha would be happier in another home, but not only was Mary very reluctant to give Risha up, there were no other homes available that would allow Risha to be an only dog. When Mary talked with Judith about the situation, Judith suggested that I might be able to help her understand what was going on with Risha by talking with her.

Mary called me and we talked at length on the phone about what was going on. I agreed to "visit" with Risha with the hope that some clarity could be achieved about how to help her.

Mary's response to what I told her after I talked with Risha was this: "What Ardeth told me was that I had a little dog suffering in silence and her outlet was going after the other dogs. I felt totally ashamed of myself. Outwardly, she would not show her pain. After getting her on several meds she was much more comfortable and tolerant."

Risha did pretty well for a while, but then the pain became too much for her again and her outbursts with the other dogs became more frequent and more severe. Risha was very loving with Mary and Dennis, but she didn't want to be around other people or other dogs at all. Any progress that had been made socially with Risha or her tolerance of other dogs totally disappeared. Mary felt like they were starting all over again. Mary worked closely with their vet, but it became clear that there was nothing more that could be done to make Risha more comfortable and they had to release her from her body.

Mary's final comments about Risha were that "Risha was a very precious little girl that had a rough life. She must have suffered in silence for years. We wanted her to feel loved and happy for whatever time she had with us. I wanted to wipe away all the bad things that had happened to her in the past, but that was not possible in her case. I came to realize she could only give so much of herself and that was okay with me. I loved it all. We have a short video showing Risha after she heard the word 'walk,' and I will always treasure that video and the completely joyful moments she would have, forgetting about all the pain and just having fun!

"I will always feel so badly that I did not understand her suffering. I want people to know there is help out there for dog owners at a loss, as I was, whether that help comes from a person like Ardeth, other medical treatments, or just talking with others. Do not hesitate to seek help.

"Risha taught me that sometimes you have to look deeper into matters that on the surface seem so clear and that even through all the pain there are simple pleasures in life that can be enjoyed, and those pleasures make life worth living. Some things we cannot change or understand but can only accept. Love is that acceptance.

"I loved her very much and so enjoyed sitting with her, just talking to her and holding her close.

Mary with Molly and Risha

"She would look at me with those big Cocker eyes and sometimes she would give kisses. I felt she knew she was loved and safe with us and that is what is important. We're very grateful to Old Dog Haven for giving us the opportunity to welcome Risha into our lives and for the support we received from them while Risha was with us. It was truly a privilege to have her as part of our family."

You might be feeling that this story hasn't provided the kind of happy ending you were hoping for, but this **is** a happy ending story in that Risha did feel loved and wanted by Mary and Dennis during the year she was with them. I know that because she told me she did. While it's true that Mary and Dennis weren't able to "fix" Risha, they did give her what was lacking in her life when she came to them: medical attention, love, acceptance, and security. Because dogs live in the moment, those gifts were valued by a little dog that went Home knowing there were people who cared about her.

LUCY AND DESI

Aunty Lucy and Desi the Peacemaker

Lucy   Desi

Sometimes saving an old dog takes more than just a phone call to Old Dog Haven from a shelter. It's really never that simple, but in this story two wonderful old dogs would never have been rescued at all if someone not directly connected to Old Dog Haven hadn't intervened on their behalf.

Many people who see a dog living in less than desirable conditions don't have the courage and determination to do anything about what they see. Now, when I say "do anything" I'm not talking about stealing the dog away in the middle of the night. I'm thinking about a more legal approach like talking to the people who live in the house, leaving food and water for the dog, calling Animal Control, or notifying a rescue group to see if the dog can be taken in **if** the dog's people are willing to surrender him.

We receive many calls from people who say they have rescued a dog but can't keep him and want us to take him. When we ask for verification that the dog has actually been surrendered by his/her people, sometimes that's when the story gets wonky: "No, I found the dog." "Someone gave me the dog." "I took the dog out of the yard because she was being neglected." Those kinds of responses don't resolve the situation in terms of Old Dog Haven taking the dog. Old Dog Haven doesn't take in strays, nor do we take in dogs that have been taken from their homes without permission from the person legally responsible for the dog. Dogs that come to us are either surrendered by a shelter or by the people who are legally responsible for them.

Lucy and Desi, brother and sister, (Look at their matching ears!) were living under a mobile home when Marty Crowley saw them. It was clear to Marty that the dogs were being neglected so she decided to become their advocate.

Marty says, "When I saw them for the first time they were very sweet, but cautious. Lucy seemed to sense that I was on their side and was protective of Desi. Desi was very shy and didn't want to have too much contact."

Marty talked with the person who lived in the mobile home and found out that the dogs were originally cared for by someone who couldn't keep them any longer. The young man with whom Marty spoke had offered to take them. As is often true with people who have good intentions, the reality of caring for two older dogs became an issue for the young man. Initially the dogs stayed inside during the day, but the young man worked long hours and by the time he returned home the dogs had been inside too long to hold their water or maintain control of their bowels. The young man then started leaving the dogs outside all the time. He did have a dog house for them, but during the winter even that meager shelter didn't keep out the cold and wet weather.

Marty was persistent. She contacted Old Dog Haven to ask if a place could be found for Desi and Lucy if she could convince their person to release them to our custody. Judith listened to Marty talk about these two old dogs that needed not only a real home but probably medical attention as well, and she said that if the dogs' person released them to Old Dog Haven we would take them.

Only in the movies do things like this happen overnight. Marty says, "It took several conversations and supportive talks to get Lucy and Desi released. Finally, the young man acknowledged that he really couldn't adequately care for the dogs."

Several days after the young man finally realized he couldn't care for Desi and Lucy, Marty transported the dogs to Home Base with the help of an Old Dog Haven volunteer. Both dogs stayed with Judith and Lee for several days while vet visits were arranged and an assessment could be made about their health and physical condition.

Marty ends her part of this story by saying, "I can only tell you that caring for any animal in my lifetime has been a privilege. Lucy and Desi were two older dogs that got left behind and truly just needed a warm and loving home. My time with both became a spiritual journey that will be with me forever."

Other than a much needed grooming and some arthritis that could be easily managed, Lucy was in pretty good shape. She was immediately taken in by one of our foster moms, Yvonne Sauter. Desi, on the other hand, was suffering from *Pemphigus Foliaceous,* an autoimmune disorder that causes the dog's immune system to manufacture antibodies against a compound naturally found in the skin called Desmoglein I. The results are multiple pus-filled blisters that form in various places on the dog's body. In Desi's case, his face and ears were affected. He looked as though he'd been badly burned. Judith and Lee decided that Desi should stay with them so treatment could begin immediately for his skin problems.

Yvonne had planned to just foster Lucy until a permanent home could be found for her, but as is true of many of our foster moms, Yvonne became a "failed foster" and ended up adopting Lucy. She says, "I quickly realized how lucky we (she and her other dog, Flora) were to have her. For many years, life was good for me and my two girls."

Lucy's bond with Flora was immediate. Yvonne says, "The afternoon Lucy arrived we went for a ride in the car to see how she would like that. I will never forget how Flora and Lucy sat in the back seat just gazing at each other. So much love and so happy to be with each other. Lucy fit like a glove."

The bond between Lucy and Flora was also important because Yvonne's beloved dog, Bali, had died a month before Lucy came to live with Yvonne. After Bali left, Flora became sad and depressed because her dog pal wasn't physically there any longer. Yvonne says that she "just rolled up in a ball and didn't even greet me when I came home."

Yvonne says, "Aunty Lucy did an awesome job picking up where Bali left off. She did a great job raising Flora. She even played with Flora. Well, she'd pretty much just step back and forth while Flora ran around in circles."

Yvonne walked with Lucy and Flora twice a day on the trail near her house. Yvonne says, "Flora looked like a little black bear and Lucy like a large raccoon. I always got the impression they were playing cowgirls and Indians when they were running around together in the bushes."

As with so many of our dogs, Lucy became an ambassador for old dogs while she lived with Yvonne. Yvonne says, "She spread a lot of goodwill for older dogs in the neighborhood. Five neighbors ended up adopting rescue dogs, and Lucy became known as the Old Dog Haven 'I Love Lucy' pooch."

Everyone who has adopted or taken in an older dog (yours truly included) will tell you that there is much joy to be found in seeing the dog enjoy new experiences. In the case of Lucy it was swimming. Yvonne says, "Initially she was very hesitant. She'd go knee deep but only with me beside her, and that was as far as she'd go. However, by mid-summer when the weather turned hot, she got into swimming. And that was that. From that day on, Lucy LOVED to swim." Lucy probably figured out that being in the water was good for her arthritis too. Smart dog.

Smart is a word Yvonne uses often when she talks about Lucy. "Lucy was SMART. She liked to bark, especially when she was happy and excited. To tone it down, she learned 'whisper woofies,' which made a huge difference for those around her. And, because whisper woofies require less energy and strength, she was able to 'bark' until the very end."

The end for Lucy didn't come until she'd been with Yvonne for almost four years. Arthritis can only be kept at bay with medication for just so long and the walks became shorter, but Yvonne was determined that Lucy still be able to join her and Flora on their daily walks so she bought a special cart for her. Flora either helped to pull the cart or walked alongside so Lucy knew she was there.

Lucy also developed dementia, which became an even more serious issue for her than the arthritis. Her quality of life finally deteriorated to the point that Yvonne needed to say good-bye to her friend. Yvonne says, "Lucy had the loveliest smile both on her face and in her eyes. Her dementia took away that bright awareness."

I talked about dementia earlier in the chapter about Bridgette, but the topic is important enough to mention again because of the devastating effects of dementia on dogs. I talk with people every day who are struggling with the decision to release their dogs from their bodies, but many people aren't really willing to even consider euthanasia if the problem isn't physical. I do understand that it's often easier to make that difficult decision if a dog is dealing with very serious physical issues, but people often overlook the emotional and mental suffering of a dog that is experiencing dementia. Dogs, unlike many humans, want to be well and in control of their mental and physical functions. When they become confused and stressed by that confusion, their lives slip from living with awareness to just existing.

Often the early stages of dementia are tolerated by some dogs that are able to just go with the flow and not be bothered by it, but that lack of concern doesn't last very long in most cases. I once had the pleasure of knowing and loving a lovely old schnauzer named Bentley—aka "Foggy Boy." For a while Bentley wasn't really bothered by the dementia that took hold of his mind. He was a foggy boy and he didn't care. He was safe, loved and happy so it was all good. He could hardly see or hear, but his radar was very effective and he seemed to always be aware of his surroundings. But, eventually he became confused, and with that confusion came anxiety and fear because his radar was compromised by the dementia and he had no idea where he was most of the time or how to get where he wanted to go. Bentley's Final Refuge mom, Noel Kjosness, knew that it was then time to let Bentley go, just as Yvonne knew it was time for Lucy to leave her and Flora.

Yvonne says, "Even knowing how tough that last year was, I would adopt Lucy again in a heartbeat if only I'd have the opportunity. I always felt that we understood each other. I still miss my little munchkin."

But, Lucy is only half of the story of this chapter. It's time to talk about Desi and his life with Judith and Lee. Unfortunately, Desi wasn't able to stay longer than about six months before his body failed him, but what a wonderful time he had in those months!

Successfully treated over a period of weeks, the *Pemphigus Foliaceous* cleared up and Desi was a happy camper.

Desi loved the pasture, the walks in the woods, and visiting with guests, especially kids. He was a gentle soul. Judith called him "the peacemaker of the pack because if there were ever any squabbles going on with the other dogs Desi would get between them and calm things down."

Desi seemed fine, but on a routine vet check a mass was found at the base of his heart. When Judith and Lee returned home from the vet they talked about a course of action for Desi, but Desi had his own agenda.

On the day Desi left his body he came into Judith and Lee's bedroom early in the morning and climbed up on the bed, something he'd never done before. Desi first went to Judith, stretched out next to her and put his head on her pillow. Once Judith woke and reached over to touch him he stayed with her for a few minutes before he repeated the same action with Lee. After he'd spent a few minutes with Lee he wandered off and went to his own bed in the living room. Judith remembers that Desi's behavior was unusual, but not alarming because he was so calm and he was smiling.

Not long after Desi's bedroom visit Judith came out into the living room and found Desi in his bed, but he was no longer breathing. The mass at the base of his heart had taken his life, but Desi left his body peacefully after saying good-bye to the people he loved. Judith and Lee think Desi hid the growing cancer because he was happy, but eventually he couldn't hide it any longer. Judith says, "He wanted to make a graceful exit and did so. What a lovely, lovely soul."

If you look on the Old Dog Haven website, you'll see this note written by Judith under Desi's picture: "Much loved Desi laid down on his fluffy bed shortly after 2006 started and peacefully died. On New Year's Day he joined us and a few of his younger friends for a fun walk in the woods and then ADORED having some visiting kids lie with him and pet him for hours. We hope his last months were the best of his life. He helped make them great months for us."

Dogs are domesticated animals. They are not meant to live outside 24/7. They need care, companionship, warm shelter, and most of all, they need love and to feel they are valuable. Lucy and Desi got everything they needed from Yvonne and Judith and Lee.

JORDAN

Dance Like No One is Watching

Jordan at the shelter   *Jordan seven months later*

All of the dogs that come to us do so because their people can't or won't care for them. In some cases, at least the people involved have the good sense—if it can be called that—to pass the responsibility on to someone else. Many people, however, just keep dogs without really caring for them in any significant way. Who knows why? Well, of course there are reasons, but that's the subject of a different kind of book. In any case, intervention by Animal Control is often necessary to remove dogs from homes that don't provide for their needs—on any level. Many dogs that have been victims of neglect have found their way to Old Dog Haven, and this chapter is about a truly remarkable dog that gives new meaning to the word "survivor."

As tempting as it is for me to talk about Jordan, her story is best told by someone who needs to tell this story herself because she was so emotionally involved with Jordan. Here's what Valerie Watson has to say about Jordan:

"It started with a call from Judith at Old Dog Haven. She had my first foster dog. Could I go to the Seattle Animal Shelter and pick her up? All she could tell me was that the dog was hairy and had been part of a cruelty case.

"When I got there I asked for the contact person, who told me Jordan had been kept at the Humane Society longer than most dogs because she was 'evidence' needed for the prosecution of her owners. He told me that for fifteen years a neighbor had seen Jordan in the backyard without the basic needs of food, water and shelter. The neighbor had been throwing scraps over the fence but the whining and crying continued to be an everyday occurrence. Although she thought it sad, she never intervened until one Thanksgiving weekend. Jordan's owners had left town for the long weekend and when the neighbor looked over the fence, she saw they had left without even leaving a bowl of water for Jordan. She had watched the dog suffer for so many years, and she was not only skin and bones as she had always been, but now she was old too. She didn't think Jordan would survive so she finally called the police. They in turn called Animal Control and had Jordan taken away. I don't know what the outcome of that case was, and I don't want to know because the punishment could never have fit the crime.

"When we finished all the paperwork the contact person went in the back to get Jordan. For me, animal shelters are among the most depressing places on the planet so it seemed I stood there waiting and anticipating for hours but in reality it was more like twenty minutes. When the contact person finally returned, I got my first look at Jordan and was stunned. That's the only word that comes close to describing what I felt. Hairy, that was the only thing I had been told about her physically. Suddenly words like 'emaciated' or 'crippled' seemed more appropriate. How could this German shepherd be this thin after being fed by the Humane Society for a month? What could she have looked like when they picked her up? My eyes filled with tears; she looked so broken and sad.

"There was no touching scene, no instant connection, even though that was what I wanted. Jordan wanted out the door. She didn't care to meet me or say good-bye to her guardian angel: the person who had called Old Dog Haven rather than put her down. He had told me her whole fifteen years had been desperate and lonely. He wanted her to have a chance, no matter how short, to love and be loved. I told him I couldn't make any promises but my husband Cliff and I would do our best for her. Truth be told, we had never had a dog this big or sadly damaged.

"Getting her in the car was quite a challenge. I was pretty sure it was a first for her. The 45-minute drive home was unpleasant at best. Jordan sat up in the back seat, whining non-stop. I was trying not to cry. I felt overwhelmed and under qualified to take care of this dog.

"She had a great many needs, and I wondered if Judith should have called someone with more experience for a dog like this. Cliff and I had just spent several years taking care of our very geriatric Bull Dogs. They hadn't been gone long when we saw the 'Human Interest' story on the news about Old Dog Haven. We still had a 'pound puppy' at home, and even though our house is small it felt empty without the Bull Dogs. We figured we had a lot of experience taking care of old dogs and Judith needed foster parents so it would be a perfect fit. Before calling her we had that talk; you know, the one about these foster dogs are old, they won't live long and how crushing the grief can be when they die. We couldn't afford the vet expenses that go with old dogs but thankfully Judith explained that donations would take care of that. We would be responsible for food and grooming. The last hurdle for me was the word 'foster.' When I fall in love with a dog, it's with my whole heart. I couldn't bear the thought of taking care of a dog until someone else adopted her. Judith told me that there were also Final Refuge homes for dogs that were too old, sick or traumatized to be adopted. It sounded like what we were looking for, that is until Jordan was in the back seat.

"When we got home, Cliff and Kona, our other dog, came out to meet our newest family member. Jordan couldn't have cared less about any of us. Her head and tail stayed down but I tried to remind myself that was to be expected. She wouldn't look at us or respond to her name and I knew deafness wasn't one of her issues. She just wanted to go and it didn't matter where. I could only imagine what a month in a cage had been like for her. I took her for a quick walk around the block and in the house we went. As I'm sure you know, dogs love nothing better than getting to smell a new place; very few things compare to that in the joy department.

"As soon as we were inside I removed her leash and the pacing began. I tried to show her where the water was and she didn't even slow down. From one room to the next, pacing. It was clear something was wrong with her hips and her back feet would sometimes curl back like she was trying to tiptoe. We later learned from her vet that poor nutrition growing up had caused her paw problems. The pacing continued. One hour became two. I would reach out my hand and stroke her back when she walked by, but she never acknowledged my touch. She would only stop long enough to eat or when we took her outside for bathroom breaks, but the moment we walked back inside the pacing renewed. I was getting frantic and felt so inadequate. It took all I had not to call Judith and tell her I had made a mistake and was in way over my head with this one. What could I do to bring her some peace? She was so thin, even with all that hair you could see every rib. Her hip and shoulder bones stuck out sharply. What was driving her? We had gotten home at about 2:00 p.m. on a Saturday and the pacing went on for about seven hours. She finally stopped when I took a hold of her collar and very gently made her lie down on her dog bed. I stayed by her for a few minutes, petting her and promising her that life was going to get better, but when she finally looked me in the eyes, I felt like a liar.

"The next day was a Sunday, and Jordan wouldn't get up. It wasn't that she couldn't, she just didn't want to. Cliff and I made her get up a few times for bathroom breaks and tried to get her to drink a little but that was it. I of course had no way of knowing if she had just exhausted herself the day before or if she was confused and/or depressed. I went to her several times, petting her and talking to her, but something told me to give her some time and space to try and make sense of what was going on.

"It took a few days before she decided to leave the safety of the bedroom and explore her new world. It was hard not to laugh as she tried to learn how to get out of the way so doors could be opened and how things like stairs worked. Our carpet took a beating for a couple of weeks as she learned how dog doors work, but you can teach old dogs new tricks. Until then I hadn't thought about the fact that if something had not been in her old back yard she had no idea what it was or how it worked. Once her curiosity was piqued, a floodgate opened and there was no stopping her. Before, every waking moment had been devoted to searching for food and companionship; she now had both in abundance. It was so fun watching her smell or taste everything that came within five feet of her. Jordon was always on the hunt for a new experience and even at fifteen she was almost unstoppable.

"As spring turned to summer, she figured out that flowers were her favorite. She made it her job to inspect every bloom on each dahlia, and there were a lot of them, but that just made it more exciting.

"Anytime she got to meet a new person, they became her new best friend. She accepted everything as it came at her; whether it was a yes or a no, a go or stop, she embraced it all with enthusiasm.

"Very quickly, we became close. Obviously when I had to go

Jordan and Valerie in the garden

to work, she stayed home, but she wanted to be with me every moment possible and the feeling was mutual. It's not possible to put into words the bond that developed between Jordan and me. I can only guess that because she had been so lonely all her life her intense need to be with me and be loved stemmed from that. I have had dogs my whole life and I have loved every one of them, but it was just somehow different with Jordan.

"After about three months we took her for a recheck at the vet because she had been such a mess physically and they wanted to keep an eye on her progress. No one believed it was the same dog! At first the ladies in the office thought I was trying to play a joke on them because no dog could change that much in such a short time. Her head was up; her tail was wagging as if we had been together her whole life. She had gained weight and her coat and eyes were bright and shiny. It wasn't until they watched her walk, with the limp and those curling up toes, that they believed it was really her.

"While Cliff and I worked, Jordan had Kona and the love of her life, Angus, to keep her company. Angus, a big lab mix, belonged to our neighbor and he stayed at our house about thirteen hours a day, usually seven days a week. We had made this arrangement with our neighbor so Angus wasn't stuck in a pen all day and he and Kona could keep each other company. The neighbor had a key to our back yard and each morning he would put Angus back there. Angus would run through the dog door making sure everyone knew he was "home." Jordan was in love. Poor Angus; after Jordan joined our family, the minute he'd run inside she would put her face right next to his and bark for two to three minutes straight. It was as though she was screaming, "I love you! I love you! I love you!" over and over again. Angus would half-close his eyes and just wait for it to be over. Her enthusiasm and love for him was out there for the whole world to see; there was nothing "stand offish" about her.

"We would play catch with Angus, and because he was young and strong, he always got the ball before Jordan could even get close, but her happiness came from chasing Angus. Her hips slowed her way down but she put everything she had into it.

"Days, then weeks, then months flew by as they always do. Just to watch her, day in and day out, enjoying anything and everything that came her way was a joy. She became a sponge looking for and soaking up all life could offer her. When new people would meet her they would often ask about how old she was, the usual questions. At first I enjoyed telling her story because she was such an inspiration. But it always got twisted. People would want to tell me how kind I was for taking her in and that wasn't even close to right. When I tried to explain it sounded like false modesty.

"We had a wonderful year with Jordan, watching her have so much fun and making us laugh just about daily at the situations her curiosity got her into. But the day came as we knew it would; her hips were worn out. Getting up and around was getting too difficult. Even with pain medication she was obviously becoming very uncomfortable. I called the vet and made her last appointment. I honestly think it was one of the best times she ever had, lying on the table, getting hand fed treat after treat. I sat on a chair so we were eye to eye with me talking to her, telling her how very much she was loved and was going to be missed more than I could say. I also told her I believed I would see her again one day. After she died, I gave her a last kiss and hug. I clearly remember wishing I could make my love for her stop when her heart did.

"It's been a few years but I still grieve for, and miss her.

"I don't know where to begin when I think about what Jordan taught me and I hate sounding like a cliché, but I think it starts with forgiveness. I tried to always be a forgiving person but the way she forgave human beings for fifteen years of horrible neglect is beyond anything I had personally experienced. Not only forgive but truly and wholeheartedly, let it go. And no matter how old I am, it's never too late to embrace life and savor each moment. Jordan embodied that saying "Dance like no one is watching." Who would have thought I would be lucky enough to get a four-legged soul mate too?

"Because Jordan was so amazing, she made it easy for us to open our home to more Old Dog Haven dogs. I doubt there will ever be another like her but each has been special in a different way. I cry and am sad when each dog passes but I wouldn't trade the experience because for each negative there are countless positives. So many sad stories with happy endings, but mostly it's about the love."

BEAUREGARD

A Joyful Spirit

As you've seen from the previous chapter about Jordan, dogs are amazingly resilient.

Somehow, in spite of whatever kind of abuse or neglect dogs have experienced, many of them are able to enjoy life and be happy if their circumstances change. Time and time again we take in dogs that don't look or act like they'll be able to stay in their bodies very long, but something wonderful happens when somebody loves and cares for them. They respond to love, kindness and medical attention by doing their best to be well, and they live far longer in their old bodies than we would think possible.

Beau, a bit like the Energizer bunny, kept on going, and lived until he was over nineteen years old. He was sixteen when he came to us and he lived happily with his Final Refuge mom, Rhonda Rowe, for more than three years. This is Beau's story.

Many people are breed-specific in their preference of dogs. Others aren't so much interested in one particular breed, but they do have strong feelings about breeds they **don't** like very much. Rhonda Rowe, Beau's Final Refuge mom, says, "If I had been asked if there was a particular breed of dog that I didn't care for, hands down I would have said poodles. Foo-Foo, prissy, fluffed and coiffed dogs were not my idea of wonderful dogs. I thought this was my iron-clad idea on the breed. This was all before I met Beau."

Beau was turned into the Seattle Animal Shelter by a man who didn't want him because his kids "weren't taking care of the dog." Children were expected to care for and assume total responsibility for a 16-year-old dog.

To say that Beau hadn't been cared for was an understatement of gigantic proportions. Beau was extremely thin, so matted that he could hardly see, one hind leg was so twisted in mats he could barely walk, and his toenails were growing into his paw pads and rotting. Still, he wagged his tail at everyone.

Needless to say, Beau spent several hours at the groomer after he was taken from the shelter by Rhonda, and she says that he "barely grumbled at the discomfort." Not surprising. Even though the grooming process was extensive, Beau knew that someone was trying to make him more comfortable.

When Rhonda brought Beau home after his grooming marathon, he wagged a greeting to all of the other canine and feline residents and made himself right at home. Rhonda said, "it seemed like he had already been here forever."

Because he was already sixteen, Rhonda thought she'd only have him with her for a few months, especially after a grueling, but necessary dental procedure, but Beau had other ideas.

Beau had several teeth removed. When Rhonda brought him home from the vet clinic, her initial thoughts were that he wasn't going to live long and they shouldn't have put him through the extensive dental procedure. "He was so very bedraggled and pathetic looking. His tongue stuck out and he really looked sad."

Again, Beau proved her wrong. The day after his dental, Beau was alert and back to his playful, fun self. Rhonda remembers "he rebounded amazingly. His tongue would continue to stick out as if he were sticking his tongue out at the world for all the unkindness the world had shown to him thus far. The tongue became his trademark and made him appear to be a cute little stuffed animal in his pictures. When people saw him in person they thought he was a young puppy due to his tiny frame and spunky demeanor."

How does a dog go from being called "bedraggled," and "sad," to being described as "spunky," "playful," and "fun"? You know the answer.

Over the next few years, Rhonda took in several more little old male poodles and her home became "Old Poodle Haven." Rhonda became a poodle fan "all because of my beloved Beauregard. All of the poodles have been wonderful little beings, but none have captured my heart as thoroughly as Beau. I knew that I would have a very hard time recovering from the loss of this special guy when the time came."

Each year that Beau not only lived but thrived and showed such spunk and personality, Rhonda almost believed that Beau might be immortal. He was never sick, and at each yearly exam, the vets would be amazed at his vigorous health and strong heart.

At age nineteen, Beau was still going strong. He was slated to be the poster dog at our auction in 2010 for being the oldest and one of the worst cases of neglect on intake, but sadly, a week before his debut, Beau started to get sick. He aspirated and could not clear his lungs. His immortality in this body was not to be after all.

Rhonda says, "The loss of Beau was absolutely crushing; so much so that I almost wanted to throw in the towel and discontinue working with senior dogs. However, since there were so many waiting in shelters that needed a safe place to go I went on to help the next one in need."

There will never be another Beau for Rhonda. His pictures are plastered all over her office, his collar is attached to her key ring, and his soul still lives within her heart. The emotions that are stirred by memories of him are still very strong.

Beau was truly a wonderful ambassador for neglected and very geriatric dogs that can have amazing lives no matter how little time they have left. For Rhonda, "the pleasure of meeting Beau and being able to care for and love him truly outweighs the pain of loss. Beau-Beau, rest in peace. I will love you forever."

Beau and Rhonda

SHELBY I

"She showed me how being stubborn helps one survive."

Many of the old dogs rescued from shelters in western Washington by Old Dog Haven come from The Humane Society for Tacoma and Pierce County—the largest animal welfare organization in the state of Washington. This shelter has a reasonably high adoption rate, but as with most shelters, not for senior dogs. Fortunately, the old dogs at the Tacoma shelter have someone looking out for them; many senior dogs from this shelter end up in homes provided by Old Dog Haven because of the efforts of one woman: Erica Stewart.

Erica has been volunteering at the Tacoma shelter since 2004—right about the time that Judith and Lee created Old Dog Haven, and as you may recall, she delivered Ellie to Judith and Lee. Over the years, Erica's "title" at the shelter has become "Volunteer Rescue Coordinator." Erica knows that old dogs don't get adopted from shelters, so she patrols the corridors of the shelter looking for senior dogs that might benefit from Old Dog Haven's particular brand of TLC. She talks with the shelter vet to determine whether the dog is healthy enough to be either adopted from a foster home or placed in a Final Refuge home for hospice care, and she spends time with the dog.

Once Erica gathers all information available on a specific dog she contacts Judith, who then works with our Placement/Transport Coordinator, Tina

Nabseth, to see if we have a place for the dog. And, as is so often true of volunteers, if a place isn't immediately available, every so often Erica brings the dog to her own home, either as an actual adoption or as a foster dog for Old Dog Haven.

Okay, that brings me to Shelby I, the dog featured in this chapter. It's another sad beginning, but there's a happy ending, thanks to Erica.

Shelby lived in a rental house with her people. The people left, but they abandoned Shelby inside the house. They tied her to the refrigerator and walked away. Eventually the owner of the house was notified, and his daughter took Shelby to the shelter. That's all Erica knew when she met Shelby. Later, she learned more about the situation.

When Erica noticed Shelby at the shelter she says, "My heart broke. She was so depressed and wouldn't move. I didn't know her story at that point, but I thought her people would surely show up to take her home. Little did I know that her owners were total dirt bags who had tied her to a refrigerator and left her."

Predictably, no one came for Shelby, and eventually she became more responsive to staff and volunteers as she regained her strength and realized that some people did care about her.

Shelby's number one fan was Erica, but just seeing Shelby at the shelter wasn't enough for Erica. Or for Shelby. You know what comes next … Erica asked Judith if she could foster Shelby for Old Dog Haven. A done deed.

Several months after Shelby moved in with Erica and her husband, Bob, Erica and Shelby were visiting a local dog park where they met two people who recognized Shelby. They'd heard Erica calling to Shelby and immediately came over and introduced themselves. As it turns out, this wonderful couple had actually saved Shelby's life. They lived near the house where Shelby had been abandoned, and they could hear her barking incessantly. They looked in the window and saw that the dog was tied to a refrigerator and the house had been abandoned. They called Animal Control, but nothing could be done until the owner of the house was notified. The good Samaritans broke the window and saw to it that Shelby had food and water until the owner's daughter finally brought Shelby to the shelter, which took days.

As time passed, Erica and Shelby became very close, and Erica knew that Shelby needed to be with her permanently. Erica says, "The only Christmas present I wanted that year was for my husband to adopt Shelby for me. Since we couldn't be apart, Bob and Judith gave her to me for Christmas."

When Erica remembers Shelby, she does so with a big smile on her face and a kind of stream-of-consciousness narrative about Shelby emerges:

"Shelby did crazy little dances. She would bounce up and down on her front paws out of happiness. She was a hoot.

"Every morning she woke me up by shoving at my hand until I noticed her.

"She was the most stubborn dog I've ever met, but one would have to be stubborn to have lived the life she lived and survived.

"Her other quite odd interest was Walmart. She always knew when we were approaching a Walmart and she would get so excited. Naturally, I would have to stop to let her out to pee.

"She loved going to the beach and running with the other dogs.

"She loved me to the end."

Shelby lived happily with Erica, Bob and five other dogs for almost three years before her failing 17-year-old body gave up on her and she needed to be released from the physical limitations that so reduced the quality of her life. Even now, many years later, Erica says, "We miss her and all her quirky ways."

Thank you, Erica, for all you do to help old dogs. I'm sure that Shelby does her happy dance every time you see to it that another shelter dog finds a home with Old Dog Haven. Paws up to you!

Shelby and her dog family: Back Row (L-R) Jeanie, Allie, Rocky, and Shelby. Front Row (L-R) Izzie and Rosie

MAX

"… a goofy, laid back guy."

Small children and dogs—especially older dogs—often do very well together **if** the adults in the family teach the children, regardless of their ages, how to relate to an older dog. But, if adults don't take the time to work with children on proper "old dog etiquette" there could be trouble.

We've taken in many dogs over the years that have become expendable because people surrendering the dog to a shelter say things like, "The dog doesn't get along with our toddler." Or, the dog becomes a casualty of a busy household because, "We have a new baby and don't have time for the dog."

Children can be taught how to interact with dogs, especially older dogs that might require a bit of quiet time in their lives, but these lessons demand patience and sometimes it's just easier for parents to abdicate their responsibility when it comes to caring for an older dog.

Because of what I've described in the above paragraphs we're very reluctant to adopt older dogs to families with very young children, or to a couple expecting a baby. We've seen far too many cases like the dog you're about to meet and want to be sure our old guys are matched up with people who will love and nurture them for the rest of their lives and won't send them away if the family dynamics change.

Max, a lab-shepherd mix, was what I call a "kid casualty." He was surrendered to a shelter because he supposedly didn't get along with the small children in the house. Because he was a neglected senior, Old Dog Haven was called, and Max soon found himself in a Final Refuge home with Janice Kugler and her family.

Janice became a part of the Old Dog Haven family when she saw one of our brochures at the veterinary clinic where she had taken one of their cats. When Janice talked with her kids about Old Dog Haven they all agreed that they wanted a dog, but they also knew they didn't want a puppy. "Old Dog Haven seemed like the solution to us. We would be able to help out an old dog, have the companionship of the dog in return, and give back."

When Max came to live with Janice he joined Bruno, the first dog Janice had taken in as a Final Refuge dog after learning about our organization. "Max seemed to fit, and the two get along really well. Max is the goofy, laid-back guy and Bruno is the more stoic of the two."

When Max came to Janice he had an infected ear, and hair loss on his stomach, inner back legs and throat. His skin was black. Frequent medicated baths helped Max's skin heal and now he does have hair under his chin, but not much on his legs and stomach. As is so often true, Max handled the frequent baths really well because he knew Janice was helping him to feel more comfortable. Janice says, "It's too bad people think they can ignore an animal's needs. He obviously had been neglected before being turned over to the shelter."

Interestingly enough, this "goofy, laid back guy" has had no problems getting along with all humans, young or old, since he came to live with Janice. He loves the kids, especially one of Janice's daughters, is happy to greet friends who come to visit, tolerates the cats that want to share his bed and wash his paws, can often be found snoozing in the laundry basket, and loves to go for rides in the car.

Max and his matching cat

Janice says, "At some time he must have been a ride-along buddy. He loves to be in the car, and will climb in and take a nap while we work in the yard. He sometimes goes to work with one of my daughters. When you rattle your car keys, he heads for the door."

Janice describes Max as a "bit of a Velcro dog. But, on the flip side he also seems to go with the flow. Maybe it's a lab thing, like thinking he's starving when he just had breakfast."

It's wonderful to know that a dog that was turned into a shelter supposedly because he didn't get along with children has found a forever home where he "fits right into our family." Instead of being rejected because the adults who surrendered him didn't think he belonged with them any longer, he now lives with people who love him and have offered him an opportunity to be happy.

Final note: Not long after I wrote this chapter Janice sent me an email in which she told me that Max had died of kidney failure, just two months after his best pal, Bruno, left his body. Janice says, "Max really missed his buddy after Bruno died. He had a very good life until the last day, just like Bruno did. We got to hang out in the yard and he rolled around on the grass, something he really liked to do. He did not let us know it was time for him to leave until we were all home and he could say a proper good-bye."

RUFUS

"He made so many people smile."

Rufus, an ancient, chocolate labrador retriever, was so weak he needed a sling to be moved from the shelter to the car of the transport volunteer who would be bringing him to Judith. Because Rufus very clearly needed to see a vet right away, the transport volunteer brought him to the vet office where Judith met them.

When Rufus arrived at the vet clinic he could sit, but not stand. When the vet came out to see him she burst into tears. He was emaciated and had a permanent head tilt. But Rufus wagged his tail and grinned at everyone.

The initial thought about why Rufus was so emaciated was that he either had cancer or he just needed more food. The vet thought that the head tilt was most likely a brain tumor, but it could have been an inner ear infection or the remaining symptoms of a stroke. In any case, after his exam, Judith got him in her car and brought him to Home Base to live with them.

Judith and Lee started Rufus on steroid therapy and began to feed him healthy food that would help him gain strength. How quickly he changed! The head tilt went away, he gained weight very rapidly, became much steadier on his feet, and was actually able to trot around the pasture.

This tendency for a dog that is quite ill to do well very quickly is what Judith calls the "euphoria period." She says, "They're so glad to be around people who care that their body cooperates for a while and they really are able to enjoy themselves."

Rufus, described by Judith as "extremely charismatic," loved his new home. Everyone who met him was charmed by him and each time he visited the vet for a check-up everyone there came out to greet him. He had staff and vets wrapped around his paws because he was so happy. And, as Judith says, "He was cute. There's something about an old lab that's so appealing."

After about three months, the euphoria period ended. The head tilt returned and Rufus began to stagger when he walked. The initial diagnosis of a brain tumor proved to be accurate and there were no treatment options available. Judith says, "We promised him when he came that we'd let him go peacefully as soon as the symptoms were there, but it was hard. What a grand old dog he was. He made so many people smile. He had a wonderful time with us, and we'll always remember him prancing around the pasture with a toy in his mouth and a wagging tail."

Rufus is a dog that clearly illustrates a very important belief held by Judith and Lee—and by all of our foster and Final Refuge parents. We want our dogs to know that someone thinks they're valuable. Dogs like Rufus are throw-away dogs that became expendable, for whatever reason, and it's very important to us that they're able to spend time with people who validate their importance. We always wish they could stay longer, but we understand that sometimes the physical damage is too severe to reverse and we just cherish and care for them as long as they are with us. It's actually amazing that Rufus lived as long as he did, but knowing that someone loves you and cares about you makes a huge difference—whether you're a dog or a human.

Dogs process everything from an intuitive, emotional point of view, which makes it possible for what I call the "heart-body" connection to have a strong effect on them. Because they don't intellectualize, and consequently don't have a tendency to over-analyze, their perception is pure and they always get what's really going on. Rufus most certainly knew that something was wrong with him, but he didn't waste time thinking about it; he just felt happy at Home Base, loved by Judith and Lee, and he stayed as long as he could. Another important lesson taught by a dog.

MOLLY

"... an absolute joy ..."

When two people separate themselves from each other—through divorce or the dissolving of a partnership—the experience is usually very difficult for everyone involved. The household is disrupted, tension and stress are common consequences, children feel torn in their allegiance, and the separation generally is one that takes adjustment and involves a learning curve that isn't always easy. If there is a family dog, the dog is sometimes a casualty too if neither adult is willing or able to continue caring for the dog.

Old Dog Haven was contacted about Molly, a blind lab that was being staked outside in her yard for long periods of time while her male human companion was at work. The husband and wife had recently divorced, the wife had moved, the husband was planning to move soon and was more than happy to re-home Molly because he said that he couldn't take her with him. You know what happened next.

Paula Jennings, a long-time volunteer at the Everett Animal Shelter, heard about Old Dog Haven and emailed Judith expressing an interest in providing a home for a Final Refuge dog. Judith told her about Molly and Paula picked her up and brought her home.

Paula remembers that Molly "climbed right into my car and nuzzled me from the back seat on the ride home." Even though Molly couldn't see Paula, she knew she was safe and wouldn't have to spend any more time being chained outside in the yard.

Just in case you're wondering how Molly did in her new surroundings, here's what Paula had to say about the initial experience: "Once home, I leashed Molly to me (as suggested by Judith) and we spent the better part of the day walking around the house and yard so she could adjust to her new living space. She did this quite well and now navigates extremely well, relying on her nose, ears and sense of touch to guide her."

Molly has really become a poster girl for the idea that you **can** teach an old dog new tricks. When Molly came to Paula she had a history of less than friendly behavior toward cats ... and even other dogs. Paula, an instructor of the feline and foster provider classes at the Everett shelter, also fosters cats. Paula was determined to make it work with Molly so "after trying some private training lessons and basically immersing her in cats and introducing her to other dogs by walking with them first, Molly has come full circle and can hang with any and all cats that come her way, even the hissy ones."

Molly and her new friend, Milly

Molly does well with other dogs now too. She even keeps her cool when she's around small yippy dogs, and she sits quietly in the vet's office even when she's surrounded by other dogs.

Molly loves to walk, but the walks have become shorter over the last year because she has arthritis in her left hip and lower spine. She also enjoys car rides, and Paula and her husband make it a point of rolling the window down for her, even in cold, rainy weather because she loves to hang her head out and "catch the wonderful air and scents that come her way."

Another aspect of her life that's important to Molly is food. Paula says, "A favorite part of her day is the three-times-daily eye drops she receives for early stage glaucoma and inflammation from her retinal atrophy and cataracts, only because a treat is waiting for her once the drops are administered. She sits patiently each and every time knowing her reward is due."

Molly has been with Paula and her husband since late February 2010 and she continues to be a happy, well loved dog. She even received a bit of media attention when she was featured in the November/December 2010 issue of *AARP The Magazine* in an article encouraging senior citizens to foster senior dogs.

I should also mention, because this is quite unusual, the man who surrendered Molly to Old Dog Haven hasn't forgotten about Molly. In fact, he emails Paula on a regular basis requesting updates about Molly. He knew that he couldn't care for her, but he didn't just give her away and forget about her.

So, that's our girl, Molly. Paula says, "She continues to be an absolute joy for my husband and me. We're thankful she has come into our lives and are grateful for the wonderful work that Old Dog Haven does."

We're grateful too, Paula. If it weren't for people like you we couldn't possibly do what we do and Molly might never have had a second chance at happiness.

Additional note: In May 2012, after two wonderful years with Paula and her husband, it was time for Molly to leave her body. Gastrointestinal problems and Addison's disease began to seriously compromise her mobility, and the best efforts of Paula and the vet weren't enough to maintain Molly's quality of life. She was no longer comfortable in her body.

When I talked with Judith about Molly she said, "Paula and her husband put an amazing amount of effort into caring for Molly. She saw specialists and spent many hours at her regular vet clinic, took meds continually, had repeated bouts of diarrhea and GI pain, which Paula and her husband would deal with diligently. Paula and her husband went far beyond what we would have expected, but Molly was cherished and respected and her personality really flourished. The blindness became a complete non-issue."

Here's one last memory of Molly that will make you smile and will also tell you how much of a non-issue her blindness really was: Every morning Paula would walk Molly to the neighborhood espresso stand, which was located across several street intersections. One morning, Molly somehow got through the front gate and decided to go and get a latte herself. Paula frantically looked for Molly and eventually ended up at the espresso stand, where she found her. The baristas had recognized Molly and kept her with them because they knew Paula would be looking for her. I don't know whether Molly had Chai tea or an Americano, but I'm sure there was a treat involved. Quite an amazing adventure for a blind dog!

STANLEY

"My Forever Dog"

Judith and Lee have loved—and continue to love—every dog that has come to live with them, but Stanley was special. He was, according to Judith, "the dog of a lifetime."

By the time Stanley came to live at Home Base in October of 2004 in the very early days of Old Dog Haven he'd already been a "guest" of two shelters. Finally, Stanley's shelter days ended on October 22, 2004, when he and Judith met. Judith hadn't come to the shelter to meet Stanley because she didn't even know he was there, but when she saw him she asked to spend some time with him in the "meet and greet" area. Judith thought Stanley was "really nice" and he obviously felt the same about her because he refused to go back into his kennel after he and Judith had spent time together. Clearly Stanley had chosen Judith as his person, so she sat with him in the kennel area while Lee went to the front desk and filled out paperwork so Stanley could go home with them. The bond between Judith and Stanley was created at that first meeting and continued throughout the almost four years Stanley lived at Home Base.

Stanley was ill when Judith brought him home. A trip to the vet happened quickly, and it was determined that Stanley had contracted kennel cough, which had turned into pneumonia. Kennel cough can be particularly dangerous for senior dogs and must be treated early or serious complications can develop. Part of the treatment involved taking Stanley to the vet office every day for a week so he could receive fluids. Each day Judith stayed with him while fluids were being given. Everyone at the vet office thought Stanley was going to die, but Stanley tapped into his inner reserve of strength—something he did often during the following years—and he improved enough for Judith to become hopeful that he would be able to stay with her for a long time.

Stanley was always with Judith. Together they made many personal appearances. Stanley would spend hours meeting people and acting as the official Old Dog Haven Ambassador. He went to doggie class and agility class, where Judith says he "was so much better at agility than the other dogs. When we did agility he was much quicker to learn than the others, including the goldens. He loved the teeter-totter! We stopped when classes progressed to a lot of jumping, which was too hard on those very arthritic joints and back, but until that point, my 12-year-old hobbling, stiff old man was the star of the class. Boy, we had a good time." Stanley also traveled with Judith when she picked up new dogs, always reassuring the new dog that everything would be okay.

Patience was one of Stanley's many attributes. He tolerated young children running around, and was always very gracious when kids came up to meet him. Along with patience, Stanley displayed a quiet wisdom that seemed to radiate on every level.

Because Stanley did anything Judith wanted him to do, she and Lee were hoping he would become the pack leader at Home Base, but Stanley declined. He was fine with being the "senior" dog, but it wasn't in his nature to be the alpha pack leader. He left that job to Queenie.

Stanley's initial physical exam revealed that he'd had one knee surgery, and as time passed his other knee and an elbow became very arthritic. But Stanley was always able to power through his mobility issues. He became quite lame, but he was strong enough to move past the discomfort.

Walking the horse trails at the tree farm was (and still is) a favorite activity for Judith and Lee. When they're able to carve out a little time for exercise beyond their own pasture, they take as many dogs to the tree farm as are able to manage the walk. Stanley was able to do the walk until a few months before his body failed him. He loved being around the horses they saw at the tree farm, and he had no difficulty learning all of the trails.

Stanley liked the beach too, and I have many fond memories of seeing him run (and later just walk) on the beach here on Whidbey when Judith and

Lee came to visit. There's nothing more wonderful than seeing an old lab in the water having a good time, and Stanley always made me smile because he knew how to enjoy himself. Even in his last year, when he was quite lame, he did the best he could to enjoy the experience. After our beach walk, Judith and Lee would often come to my house for coffee, and it was fun seeing Stanley be his marvelous, gracious self as my noisy schnauzers swirled around him. I can still see him lying on the deck in the sun … quiet and peaceful. I liked being around him, and I miss seeing him. He was unflappable. I remember too that Stanley wore a red collar. I haven't seen a red collar on any dog at Home Base since Stanley left.

In July 2008, it was time for Stanley to leave. A tumor growing around his heart caused him to go downhill quite rapidly. Needless to say, the decision to let Stanley go was a very, very difficult one for Judith. However, as always, she knew his quality of life was more important than anything else and was able to move past her own impending sense of loss to help her friend leave his body.

For Judith, Stanley was "the best dog on earth. I still miss him; I've never gotten over him. His spirit will stay here to help all the new arrivals."

SHAWNEE TU

A Princess, not a Prince

Many times a dog is surrendered to a shelter by his or her people because the dog has health issues the people either don't want to deal with, or they can't afford the necessary medical treatment for the dog. Often, when a dog is brought to a shelter the person giving up the dog isn't honest about the extent of the medical issues involved. People would like to think that the dog they bring to a shelter will be adopted from the shelter and live happily ever after with someone else assuming responsibility for the dog, and they don't want to tell the shelter about any health issues because they're afraid those problems will prevent someone adopting the dog.

Incontinence is a good example of a condition not usually mentioned by people when they give up a dog. Nothing is said about the dog peeing all over the house. Who wants to adopt a dog that isn't housebroken? Yet, in many cases this behavior is exactly why the dog is being taken to a shelter. Somehow, in the mind of a person who is comfortable abdicating his or her responsibility, it's just easier to have the dog become someone else's responsibility rather than find out why the dog is incontinent and treat the problem. Many dogs that come to Old Dog Haven have health issues we don't know about when they're taken into our care. It doesn't really matter in the long run because we take care of whatever is going on, but it would be very helpful if we had accurate health information up front.

To say that the information we received about Shawnee Tu was inaccurate is an understatement. I'm talking basic stuff here—not rocket science medical diagnosis. Just keep reading and you'll see what I mean.

In 2009, Katie and Ben Parries were finally ready to welcome a new dog into their family. It had been two years since their beloved Shawnee, a little Yorkie that had been with them for ten years, had died. Ben and Katie started looking on the Internet and found Old Dog Haven's website. They were looking for another female Yorkie so they filled out an application to become Final Refuge parents and sent it in to Judith.

About two weeks later, Judith contacted Katie and Ben, letting them know that there was a male Yorkie named Little Bear that needed a home. Even though Katie and Ben really wanted a female, they agreed to take Little Bear and transportation was arranged.

One of our dedicated transport volunteers picked Little Bear up from the shelter and met Katie and Ben in the Chehalis Walmart parking lot.

Here's Katie's memory about what happened:

"We got there about the same time as the young lady who was delivering the dog. My husband noticed the dog squatted to go potty, but I know some male dogs do this and some females hike their leg, so I didn't think anything of it. Until I picked up the dog. When I picked him up I knew that he was a female! I told the young lady that he was a she, and she said, 'Really? I was told that Little Bear is a male.'"

And so the game of "Who's on first?" began. The transport volunteer made a phone call and talked with someone at the shelter who checked Little Bear's records and verified that he had been declared a male dog when he was surrendered. Actually, she said he'd been surrendered two times, by two different people, and in both cases he was identified as male. The transport volunteer then called Judith, who called the shelter to see if the right dog had been released to Old Dog Haven. Judith couldn't reach anyone at the shelter who knew anything about the dog, so she told Katie and Ben to go ahead and take the dog. She would call them as soon as she was able to reach someone at the shelter who could help her. As Katie and Ben were driving home with Little Bear, Judith called and said that they did have the right dog.

Really? Somehow, the person who originally surrendered the dog, the person who adopted the dog from the shelter and then returned "him," shelter staff, **and** the vet who examined the dog had all declared her to be male. How's that for inaccurate information?

Katie's response? "I told my husband that our Lord knew we wanted a female so He changed the sex. LOL."

So, Little Bear became Shawnee Tu. She was thin, matted, and Katie says she "acted like she had never had any loving human contact, which was very sad. She was blind, and we noticed when she ate she would sneeze and snort, so we took her to our vet the Monday after we got her."

When Katie and Ben took Shawnee to their vet, blood was drawn, and the vet discovered that she had a mouth full of rotten teeth as well as two fistulas that were open to her sinus cavity. The teeth needed to be pulled and the fistulas needed repairing to prevent food and water from getting into her sinuses. Judith was informed, and she arranged an appointment for Shawnee with a vet in Tumwater.

Once Shawnee had a more thorough exam in Tumwater it was discovered that there were three open fistulas instead of two, and she had a broken jaw. Surgery couldn't safely be performed until a course of antibiotics was given, so two weeks later Katie and Ben brought Shawnee back to Tumwater for surgery. When they took her back for a follow-up check a week later, the vet saw that one of the fistulas hadn't healed properly. Another course of antibiotics was prescribed. Two weeks later Shawnee was back at the vet and going through the whole procedure all over again.

Shawnee was also incontinent, so Katie and Ben would take her out every twenty or thirty minutes, and put little puppy diapers on her at night because she slept with them in their bed. They could have crated her, as many people might do, but these two caring people felt that Shawnee needed to be close to them, and they were willing to do whatever it took to make her comfortable.

Finally, Shawnee started feeling better and her personality came through in what Katie describes as "many cute ways. Her little tongue hung out because she didn't have many teeth and her jaw had been broken. I think she finally knew someone truly loved her and would take care of her."

Shawnee was only able to stay with Katie and Ben for six months before her kidneys shut down and Katie and Ben had to release her from her body. But what a wonderful six months it was for this little throw-away dog that became a Princess because two people cared enough for and about her to help her be as healthy as she could be given the limitations of her physical body.

Katie says, "I will have to admit it was a lot of time and patience but she was definitely worth it because this little dog passed knowing she was loved.

Shawnee with Katie and Ben

"One thing we would like to say to people who are skeptical about taking in blind and/or deaf dogs. We would like to assure them that the dogs' noses work very well and it's amazing how well they can get around. They just need to be watched carefully when they're outside. They give such unconditional love back to you because most of them have not had the love you are giving them."

Because of their experience with Shawnee Tu, Katie and Ben are now committed to helping senior dogs that come to Old Dog Haven. Shawnee's legacy has been passed on in the form of another blind and deaf dog they welcomed into their home and hearts after Shawnee Tu left them. Katie and Ben say that they're very grateful Old Dog Haven is "willing to rescue dogs and find them homes," and we are even more grateful that there are people like Katie and Ben who are willing to provide an opportunity for dogs like Shawnee Tu to be happy. We couldn't possibly do what we do for dogs without our dedicated foster and Final Refuge parents, and we thank all of them for their efforts on behalf of our dogs.

RILEY

"We showed them all ..."

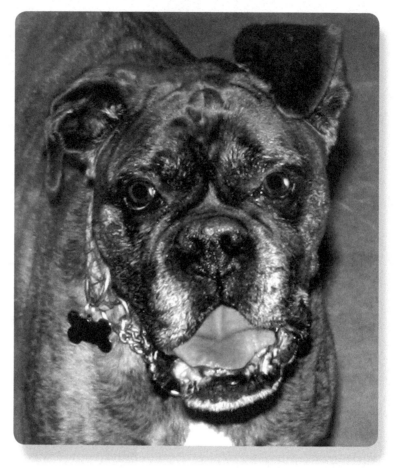

Riley was found abandoned and left to die in an empty house. Whoever had lived there moved away and left an old, sick dog to starve to death.

I wish I could tell you that this kind of thing is a rare occurrence, but unfortunately it isn't. We've had many dogs come to us from similar circumstances, (Remember Shelby?) and their stories are just as important as Riley's, but I want to tell you about Riley as a representative of this category of "How Dogs Come To Us" because he was such a remarkable survivor.

Riley was taken to a large shelter in 2008 by Animal Control. When I checked his vet records I saw words like: "emaciated" (he only weighed fifty-four pounds), "horrible shape," "large eyelid tumor," "multiple open bite wounds," "Grade 3 heart murmur," "diffusely muffled lung sounds," "severely infected with fleas," "worms," and "intestinal disease" written in the vet exam.

All in all, the vet who examined Riley was very concerned about his physical condition, and his prognosis was anything but hopeful.

But, this is a book about hope, and hope comes in many forms for some of the throw-away dogs that end up in shelters. Riley's hope came in the form of Jan Schwenger, a volunteer at the shelter.

Jan met Riley on a Sunday in April 2008 at the Tacoma Pierce County Humane Society. She and the other volunteers had finished walking the dogs, and Jan was on her way to sign out when she passed "Vet Row," a handful of kennels housing dogs that are ill and not available for viewing by the general public.

As Jan walked past the kennels something "caught my attention. I saw the cloudy eyes of a Boxer staring back at me. I stopped. He carefully began to stand, but he was barely able to get up on his wobbly legs. He was so painfully thin it made me gasp."

When Jan looked closer at the dog, she saw that he had a small tag tumor hanging off one eye, and his face was drooping on the right side from what appeared to be a past stroke. One ear fell awkwardly from massive amounts of scar tissue.

"Then," Jan said, "it started. The classic Boxer wiggle. Technically, I should not have gone back to see him, but I couldn't stop myself. I noticed he had a terrible case of diarrhea and his kennel needed attention, so I grabbed a couple of volunteers to assist me. I looped the lead over his head and took him out of the kennel while the others gave it a good cleaning. The look in those dark soulful eyes melted me.

"While he appeared to be at death's door, I could see life in those eyes. He hadn't given up; why should we? According to the kennel card he was eleven years old, which is a long life for a Boxer, but still …."

With limited staff on a Sunday there was no one Jan could talk with about the dog called Riley, but when she left the shelter she didn't forget about him.

The next day, Jan returned to the shelter and inquired about the possibility of fostering Riley. She was told that he had been found abandoned in a home by Animal Control, and based on his medical evaluation he really didn't have long to live.

Enter Erica Stewart, the Volunteer Rescue Coordinator at the Tacoma Humane Society shelter. (You met her in the chapters about Ellie and Shelby.) Erica hadn't called Judith yet about Riley, but when she knew that her friend, Jan, was interested in fostering Riley, that phone call happened immediately. Old Dog Haven came to the rescue, and Jan was able to take Riley home as a foster. Well, technically he was considered to be a Final Refuge dog because no one thought he was adoptable, but the important thing is that he went home with Jan.

Riley wasn't neutered, so after Riley gained a few very necessary pounds, Jan took him in and he came through the surgery just fine. The vet was even able to remove the eye tag, but discovered that there was cancer present in both testicles. So much for Riley being adoptable.

But wait. About a month later Jan called Judith and told her that she wanted to officially adopt Riley. (Jan is another one of those people we lovingly refer to as "failed fosters" because they end up being adopters rather than fosters.) Jan already had two large dogs at home and never planned on adding to her pack, but she couldn't resist Riley because "he had completely stolen my heart."

Every day Jan walked through the door to meet that wiggle and the wonderful smile that seemed to grow bigger each day Riley lived with Jan.

Jan and Riley took walks every day, even though Jan says, "At first I got glares by people driving by who assumed I had been starving him! We took back roads for a while until his health got better."

Jan and Riley "showed them all. Riley lived two more years with me until the cancer moved into his lungs and the day came to let him go. I feel so blessed to have had the opportunity to let him leave this life knowing love."

Riley loved rolling in the grass.

Are you smiling? You should be because you've just read about a dog and the woman who loved him who both gave new meaning to the belief that it ain't over 'til the fat lady sings.

SPARKLE

"We're so glad she graced our lives."

In 2008, the ASPCA reported that between 500,000 and one million animals were at risk of becoming homeless due to the economic crisis. In 2012, animal shelters were seeing an increase of 15-20% in animals surrendered because their people couldn't afford to keep them. When people lose their jobs and/or homes, the family dog often becomes a casualty because the money just isn't there to provide food or veterinary care.

Old Dog Haven has seen a significant increase in the number of old dogs needing homes because of the economic crisis in the past few years. Shelters and individuals call every day asking us to find homes for old dogs that have become homeless because of economic hardship. Our first priority is always to get old dogs out of shelters, but on occasion in emergency situations we have been able to place dogs that were living with individuals into our Final Refuge homes. Or, as in the case of the dog featured in this chapter, Judith and Lee have taken the dog into their own home.

Sparkle's people contacted Old Dog Haven and begged us to take her because they were about to become homeless and were unable to keep their dog. But Sparkle's story wasn't even as simple as that. The people with whom Sparkle lived weren't her first family. Apparently, Sparkle had been a kind of "neighborhood dog" and had lived somewhere else—probably many places—before the people who contacted us took her in. We didn't have any Final Refuge homes available at the time so Judith and Lee welcomed Sparkle into their own home to prevent her going to a shelter, where she most certainly would have been euthanized because of her age and physical condition.

I wish I could tell you that Sparkle arrived at Home Base as a healthy, well-loved dog, but that wasn't the case. What Judith and Lee saw was a very old, frail dog— most likely between fourteen and sixteen years old—that had been neglected for a very long time.

Interestingly, during the time Sparkle lived with Judith and Lee her people called and asked about her from time to time. They didn't seem to understand that she'd been starving; they'd actually been neglecting her while she was with them.

Sparkle's people sent along her food—a large, black garbage bag filled with rotten, moldy food—and a water bowl that was covered in green slime.

Sparkle was skin and bones. She smelled. Her fur was so matted she could barely walk. Judith remembers having to hack off the mats so Sparkle could move her legs.

The Pipers were told that Sparkle was an outside dog and she didn't like being in the house. That first night at Home Base Sparkle found a nice spot in front of the wood-burning stove, and that's where she spent most of her time for the next five months. She loved being inside.

Judith and Lee were also told that Sparkle didn't get along with other dogs, yet Sparkle was perfectly happy to be around the rest of the gang at Home Base.

Based on Sparkle's age and condition when she arrived, Judith and Lee knew she might not be with them for long, but they were determined to offer her the best care possible and to help her feel safe, loved and secure.

Judith says, "She slept a lot and moved slowly, but she was a happy dog. With medication and good care, her 'outside dog' coat began to shine and the throw-away dog she'd been when she first arrived transformed into a radiant dog. She was beautiful."

One of Judith's favorite memories of Sparkle is a "modeling session" with Karen Ducey, a photographer who came to the house wanting to take pictures of old dogs. Karen was struck by Sparkle's face and how beautiful she was. Judith remembers waiting out in the garden with Sparkle while Karen set up her equipment—a giant "umbrella" that looked like one of the old satellite dishes lined with aluminum foil. The two "after" photographs shown in this chapter were taken during that session on a summer day when a once neglected dog became a star.

Sparkle's beauty was definitely not just skin-deep. When Judith talks about Sparkle she uses words like "sweet, curious, lovely, serene, loving, and happy" to describe her.

After five months Sparkle just couldn't hang in any longer. Judith says, "Fighting her aging body had become too much of a struggle, even for this tough old lady. She left the world with those glowing eyes and a beautiful coat. Such a lovely dog. So far from the sad, dirty, thin creature she was when we took her in. We will miss her and are so glad she graced our lives."

FRED AND DUKE

Left Behind

Fred

Duke

The concept of dogs living as loved and valued family members no matter what happens often escapes people.

For some people, if circumstances change and a move is made, the dog is left behind. It's especially traumatic if the dog is an older dog that has been with the family for many years, as was the case with Fred and Duke.

Fred and Duke's human companion contacted Old Dog Haven in 2005. The woman was frantic, as people often are when they call Judith for assistance. The family was moving out of state and had decided not to bring the dogs with them. Excuses were made about why the dogs weren't welcome to join the family in their move. Judith was told that the family had tried to make other arrangements with friends and/or family to re-home the dogs, but no one was willing to take the dogs. Bringing the dogs to a shelter was the only option left until Old Dog Haven intervened and Judith was able to find a Final Refuge home for Fred and Duke with Ron Kerrigan.

Ron and I have known each other for many years, and it was no surprise to me that he immediately made places for Fred and Duke with his pack. Ron and I first met while walking dogs at the Whidbey Animals' Improvement Foundation shelter in Coupeville, before Old Dog Haven existed. He was (and still is) always willing to take in the older guys that had no chance of being adopted. Over the years, Ron has provided a Final Refuge for more than thirty dogs at his rural home. Many come with no history; some, like Fred and Duke, come with their story intact. All are loved.

Fred and Duke, both about twelve years-old, were German shepherd mix brothers that had grown up and old together. Fortunately, they were still together when their human companion brought them to Ron's home. Initially, Ron was "genuinely impressed that these were dogs that were loved. The family's little girl was in tears during the forty-five minutes we spent letting the dogs explore their new territory and meeting their new pack mates. I asked the woman to change out the dogs' tags, putting my contact information on them, and she seemed to think that made the transfer final. There were promises made by the woman who brought the dogs to me that they would keep in touch and send Old Dog Haven money regularly to support the dogs."

The minutes after a former family leaves can be traumatic for the dog left behind. Fred and Duke watched their family go out through the gate, and when Ron returned from seeing them off, the dogs were still sitting near the gate, watching and waiting. The newbies didn't show signs of distress, but Ron knew they were probably confused. So, the next half hour was spent walking around the fenced acre to which the dogs have access, and then dinner was served.

When Fred and Duke arrived, Ron had six other dogs—a mix of senior and "troubled" dogs that were not easily adoptable at a shelter. Adding two more dogs didn't seem like a big deal since Ron felt that "once you get up to six or seven, another one or two doesn't take that much more effort, except in finding corners to put their food dishes down in." The new arrivals fit in well and integrated quickly, negotiating the dog door and learning the routine Ron and his pack had developed.

Fred and Duke passed Ron's big "test" for new arrivals with flying colors. Questions on Ron's test are not: "Is the dog housebroken?" "Can the dog be left for a period of time without barking?" "Is the dog destructive?" Ron's test really only has one question: "Does the dog get along with other dogs?" Fred and Duke adjusted to their places in their new pack very well. They didn't avoid mixing, which is sometimes an issue when dogs arrive as a bonded pair. Eventually they even stopped sleeping in the same area; Fred claimed one particular corner as his own, and Duke bravely tried to snuggle with the other dogs on the bed. They also proved to be housebroken, quiet, and chewed only what was allowed. Ron says, "They proved to be very lovable."

Fred and Duke were **very** overweight when they came to Ron. The vet records provided described both dogs as "obese" and indicated that they'd been so for many years. Apparently, bowls of food were available to the dogs twenty-four hours a day, which had resulted in serious weight problems for both dogs. Fred weighed ninety pounds and Duke tipped the scale at eighty-nine pounds. With Ron's help, six months later Fred was down to eighty-two pounds and

Duke weighed seventy-eight pounds. When Fred died two and a half years after arriving at Ron's home, he weighed sixty-seven pounds.

Duke had a long history of seizures and his body was covered with large, fatty tumors. He actually looked like he was carrying saddle bags. Vet records indicated that the seizures had become more frequent, and Ron started to see them a few weeks after Duke arrived. They were probably not as severe in his former home since he had access to food all the time, but since his food was being limited, the seizures became more frequent. The seizures manifested themselves in the typical shaking, falling over, uncontrolled urinating, and a glazed look in the eyes followed by drooling, disorientation and restlessness. Duke was diagnosed with "low blood sugar," and Ron was told that he needed to have a spoonful of corn syrup every six hours to prevent a seizure, which Ron provided. (This is the kind of dedicated care that our Final Refuge parents are willing to offer our dogs on a regular basis.) Six months after arriving, Duke was diagnosed with *Pancreatic Insulinoma*, which would eventually spread to his liver. It was decided not to put Duke through surgery, and he lived another five months before he seemed to be in too much stress to continue. Ron arranged to have Duke euthanized at home with his brother, Fred, by his side.

Fred lived on in his new home, perfectly content with his new pack. Ron often took Fred to events because Fred was so mellow and had an unusual growth on his lower eyelid that always made people notice him. Fred had the usual senior issues—such as back leg problems, no doubt exacerbated by years of being overweight—and was on a regular regimen of meds to control his discomfort.

In July 2007, Fred started to develop a large lump on his right rear leg where it joined the body. A vet exam revealed that it was an osteosarcoma. Amputation wasn't a good option; Fred already had mobility issues with his back legs and couldn't handle having only one back leg. There was nothing to do but wait and watch. One day, Ron noticed a trail of blood on the floor and discovered that Fred's tumor had split open. It was one of the signs Ron had been waiting for and dreading. He rushed Fred to the vet, where Fred was sedated and then euthanized.

Two old dogs that should have ended their days here with their lifetime family were loved and cared for in their last months and years by a stranger who became their devoted friend.

Fred and Duke's bodies are buried next to each other on Ron's property underneath a native tree.

A P.S. from Ron: "Neither Old Dog Haven nor I ever heard a word or saw a dime from their former family."

As with all the dogs featured in this book, Fred and Duke left a legacy of lessons that humans might do well to learn:

- If you're planning to move or are thinking about a lifestyle change, don't rationalize not taking your dog by saying that the move would be "too hard on the dog." Dogs want to be with their people.
- If you feel that you absolutely can't take your dog with you when you move, please don't wait until the last minute to find a home for your dog. Don't expect others to step in and assume responsibility for your dog.
- Make a lifetime commitment to your dog. Don't send him or her to strangers.
- Allowing your dog to become obese causes serious health issues for the dog.
- Old Dog Haven foster parents are able to open their hearts and home to dogs that have no other options.

Fortunately, dogs live in the moment. The moments Fred and Duke spent being loved and cared for by Ron gave them pleasure and happiness. If you learn the lessons Fred and Duke's story offers regarding commitment to animals and their health care, then they can also take pleasure in knowing that their legacy provided valuable lessons for humans.

FLOWER

"Flower Power! She's taught me to never lose hope or give up on a dog."

What Old Dog Haven is able to do for senior dogs couldn't possibly happen without the efforts, dedication, and commitment of many people, illustrated so well by Flower's story. Little Flower's journey to health, safety and love was made possible by the caring people named in this story. It really does take a village!

Flower was surrendered to the Olympic Peninsula Humane Society (Pt. Angeles) in February by someone who said that Flower was an 11-year-old Shih Tzu that "should have been put to sleep two years ago because of the

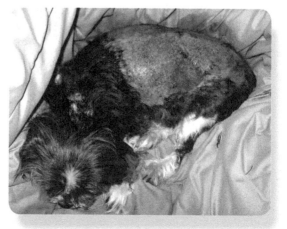

mites." The shelter manager, Dr. Suzy Zustiak, a veterinarian, was horrified at what she saw: a dog with a horribly bulging eye and nearly consumed by demodectic mange.

Adult dogs don't get demodex unless they are immune-compromised by disease or neglect. This poor little dog was truly miserable.

Dr. Zustiak contacted Old Dog Haven to see if we would be able to provide a home for Flower as well as tend to her physical needs. Our consulting veterinarian, Dr. Victoria Peterson, reviewed the information given by Dr. Zustiak and advised us about what to expect when we saw Flower.

We contacted one of the shelter volunteers, Franny Koski, who often transports dogs to us. She took Flower home overnight and then drove her many miles (including a ferry ride) to another transport volunteer, Shari Lau. Shari then brought Flower to her foster family, Kelly Marlo and her husband, Per Cummings.

When Kelly met Flower, she saw her as "a lifeless little ball of greasy matted fur, open sores, cracked skin and scabs all over her back. Her left eye was bulging, she couldn't see well and she seemed partially deaf."

The vets at our "home clinic," Frontier Village Veterinary Clinic, became involved right away because it was clear that Flower needed immediate attention. After an extensive examination, including blood work and X-rays, Flower returned home with Kelly to begin her healing process. After a month of intensive treatment with an arsenal of drugs, baths, topical treatments, good food and love, Flower's skin was much improved and she was strong enough for an initial surgery. We discovered that she had been spayed but only after multiple Caesarian sections, leaving a hernia and very damaged skin. She had been having puppies repeatedly despite her miserable physical condition.

Dr. Jared O'Connor removed enlarged lymph nodes over Flower's mammary glands. We can't be sure they aren't lymphoma (cancer) but it's likely that the nodes resulted from the long-term infection in her skin. She had an extensive dental procedure at the same time.

A veterinary opthalmologist, Dr. Terri McCalla of Animal Eye Care in Bellingham, also examined Flower and determined that the bulging eye needed to be removed. Because we'd found two different multi-drug-resistant bacteria in her ears and the surgical site, it was determined that the eye surgery needed to be postponed a few months, during which time eye drops would be administered to control the pressure and pain.

When she first arrived at Kelly's home, Flower slept for almost a month. Kelly says, "… to be honest, I've never seen a dog like this. She was very quiet, somewhat shut down, a bit of a zombie. I remembered thinking that I'd never fostered a dog that had no personality at all. She didn't want affection, didn't care about anything but a little food. She slept about twenty-three hours out of the day."

And then, as Kelly says, "the real Flower started to emerge. A little tail wag, a bit of excitement when you would come near her. A huge appetite. This little girl started barking orders, letting us know what she wanted. Slowly the hair started coming back in, her ears cleared up, and then her personality blossomed. She's a bit of a 'Goldilocks' and spends the afternoon going from the couch to every dog bed in the house, looking for the one she deems the most comfortable. She has now earned the nickname "The Little General' because we all stand up and salute when she decides to get up in the morning. And the best of all—she loves to snuggle in bed with us many mornings. It's probably been years since anyone held her, and she probably didn't receive much attention once she was done producing puppies. We're trying to make up for it, and we spend many hours spoiling General Flower rotten. We absolutely love her! We still have a lot of rehabilitation to do, but she's pulled through the worst of it. She's quite the survivor, and she has taught me never to lose hope or give up on a dog!"

The great groomers at Pawsitively Styling in Arlington gave Flower a stylish haircut (keeping the hair away from her damaged eyes) and Flower looked like this four months later.

Flower has had quite the journey since being discarded at the shelter. Seeing the happy, comfortable, confident dog that has emerged has made everyone's efforts **very** worthwhile. Thanks to all, especially Kelly and Per, for giving Flower the opportunity to be a happy, healthy little dog.

Final Note: After two and a half years of loving and being loved by Kelly and Pers, little Flower's brave heart failed her and she's no longer physically with us.

KAYCEE

"She's absolutely beautiful ... inside and out."

The Cavalier King Charles spaniel is a purebred dog you might expect to see in the show ring or, at the very least, holding court within a family setting. You probably wouldn't expect to see this breed of dog at a shelter, living in a cage. But, when it comes to people who don't want their dogs any longer, the breed doesn't seem to matter. Nor does the age or physical condition of the dog. Thousands of purebred dogs find their way to shelters every day. Just look on www.petfinder.com and you'll see what I mean. Some are surrendered by their people for various reasons, and others are found as strays and brought in by Animal Control.

KayCee is a purebred Cavalier King Charles spaniel that was brought to a shelter as a stray. Shelter staff estimated her age to be around twelve. She weighed about eleven pounds, could barely see, was severely anemic, had abscessed teeth, had never been spayed, and had a serious heart condition. It's beyond understanding that someone could just abandon this dog, but as I've said so often in this book, it happens all the time. She wasn't a lost dog that had somehow wandered off and had people who loved her frantically looking for her. No one ever claimed KayCee.

Well, that's not quite true. Old Dog Haven was called about KayCee and one of our long-time fosters, Rhonda Rowe, not only claimed KayCee, but named her as well.

Rhonda says, "I fell instantly in love with her. She was absolutely beautiful. I named her KayCee (KC for King Charles). When I first met her, I reached down to pet her head, and she cried out in pain. Her eyes hurt badly, and she was practically blind."

Rhonda immediately made a vet appointment for KayCee. Judith was there for the vet exam and says, "Her condition just horrified me. Her head was hanging down from pain, one of her eyes had ruptured from glaucoma, the other one was swollen with corneal edema, and the pain had to have been incredibly intense. She was so anemic (perhaps from flea infestation … who knows?) that they considered a transfusion, but decided to go ahead with surgery immediately to end the pain from her eyes. Her heart and the anemia made it hugely risky, but we had no choice."

The procedure of removing KayCee's badly damaged eyes went so quickly and so well that the vet decided she could also be spayed at that time. As the vet tech was shaving KayCee's stomach, she felt something odd in KayCee's belly. An X-ray was immediately taken and two perfectly formed puppies were seen on the film. Needless to say, the spay surgery didn't happen that day.

So, not only did we have a 12-year-old dog in terrible shape, we had a pregnant dog. A first for Old Dog Haven. Rhonda says, "KayCee came home with a cone around her neck so she couldn't scratch at her eyes, but she was still so beautiful. It amazed me how easily she found her way around, through the dog door and down into the yard, back up and to her favorite bed, to my desk for some snuggles, and to where her regular feeding place was. She wore the cone for ten days. On the eleventh day, she gave birth to her two puppies.

KayCee and her four day-old puppies

"KayCee did a fantastic job of birthing, cleaning and feeding her pups. The puppies didn't appear to be purebred—mixed with something black—but they were equally adorable. KayCee raised her pups to be healthy, and as sweet and even-tempered as she was herself."

Judith says, "How she survived not only the surgery but carrying puppies to full term in that condition just astounded all of us. What a survivor. What a tough little girl."

The pups were spayed at eight weeks and adopted out to wonderful homes when they were ten weeks old. Who knew that Old Dog Haven would ever be involved in puppy adoption? Rhonda says that even though KayCee was a wonderful mom, she was "very ready for her girls to leave home."

It's been almost four years since KayCee was rescued by Old Dog Haven. Her once-thin body has filled out, her coat is shiny and luxurious, her heart condition is easily managed with medication, and she no longer experiences pain from damaged eyes. Rhonda says, "it's clear that KayCee is not just a survivor, but a testament to what good care, love and attention can do for a 'throw-away' dog. Not only has KayCee thrived in her home with many other foster dogs that come and go and several cats, she's always ready for public event outings, car rides, and walks around the neighborhood. But mostly she loves the cuddling and affection her foster family subjects her to on a daily basis. She gets the award for world's best hugger. I think she's absolutely beautiful—inside and out. Sometimes, I even swear that she can see. The expressions on her eyeless face are quite dramatic and she seems to be able to look into a person's soul and understand all that is said. KayCee has touched my life and soul, that's for sure."

TEDDY

"… life is now and joy can be found when you least expect it."

Those of us who adopt senior dogs often think we're rescuing them, when in many cases—as was true with my Teddy—the dogs are doing the rescuing. Actually, it works both ways most of the time. Sometimes, however, we lose sight of what dogs offer humans on so many levels, and it takes a dog like Teddy to remind us that dogs always offer many opportunities for humans to learn, if we're up to the challenge.

My partner of forty years left her body in July of 2005. Six months later, I had to say good-bye to my long-time dog friend, Joey. Joey, as is true of many dogs, was reluctant to leave, but his body was failing him in ways that compromised his quality of life so I sent him on his way with love and thanks for a wonderful life together. Even though my other two dogs, Harper and Angus, were still with me, Joey told me that he'd send me a new friend because he knew that there would be room for at least one more dog after he left. I told him that I'd be happy to welcome any dog he sent to me, but I had no idea another dog would arrive so soon after Joey's departure.

Three days after Joey left his body, Judith called and asked me to take an 8-year-old dog that had just been through a very difficult experience. She explained that Fritz had been found sitting beside the dead body of his human companion. Apparently, a neighbor became concerned because she hadn't seen Fritz's person for several days, and when she knocked on the door there was no answer. The woman then called the police. Soon after their arrival, the coroner's van pulled up to the house. The coroner estimated that the man had been dead for four days. Four days. Fritz had been sitting with the body of his friend for four days waiting for someone to come and find him. The neighbor knew which vet the man had used so she took Fritz to the vet. The vet called Judith, and Judith called me. Judith's comment at the time, as I recall, was "this dog needs you."

As I listened to Judith talk about Fritz, a part of me wasn't quite sure I was ready to welcome another dog so soon after Joey's passing, but by the time Judith had finished her story I found myself saying that I would take him. So, Lee picked up Fritz from the vet's office and brought him to me on Sunday, January 22, 2006.

When Lee drove up to the house, I went out to greet him and my new friend. As I opened the car door to greet Fritz, I remember Lee saying, "This is a nice little dog." In retrospect, that was the understatement of the century. Fritz was sitting on the passenger seat, wagging his tail, looking all cute and fuzzy, as schnauzers do when they need haircuts. Oh, I guess I didn't mention that he was a schnauzer did I? Even though I've never been breed-specific, schnauzers seem to fall from the sky and land in my lap. Twenty of them have jumped from clouds somewhere above me during the past forty-five years. Who knows why? I guess I must send out schnauzer energy or something.

Back to Fritz. I picked him up, gave him a hug, told him I was very happy to meet him and that he was welcome here. I walked him through the gate into the yard so he could meet his two brothers, Harper and Angus. Lee and I watched as the boys played meet and greet. Then, after introductions had been offered, Fritz ran around the side of the house, up on the deck and into the house through the sliding door. Lee and I followed as Fritz immediately ran into the bathroom to get a drink. He knew where the water bowl was. In fact, he knew where everything was in the house. The toy basket sits by the sliding door and after Fritz had finished his drink he dived into the basket, brought out Joey's favorite toy and set it down in front of me. Then he jumped into the dog bed that had been Joey's. By this time, Lee and I were standing in the kitchen while I made tea. Fritz joined us there and immediately stood in front of the dog cookie bowl that was sitting on the counter. He couldn't see it; he just knew where it was. After he ate his cookie, he went into my study and curled up for a minute on the dog bed that had been Joey's favorite place to hang out when I was working at the computer. (I've taken a page from

Judith and Lee's decorating style in terms of a house full of dog beds.) Angus and Harper acted as though Fritz had always been there, and soon all three of them were in the living room with Lee and me. I was sitting on the hearth, and before I knew it Fritz hopped up on my lap, gave me a big wet kiss, looked at me and said, "I'm here for you. Let's get on with our lives." No, he didn't use words. Dogs don't need words to communicate, but the message was as clear as if he'd actually spoken to me.

If you're thinking that Joey had come back to me in Fritz's body, you'd be wrong. It doesn't work that way. But, what was clear, and later explained by Fritz, was that he and Joey had talked and Joey had told him that he'd be coming to live with me. Joey also did some coaching about where everything was in the house, including his favorite toys, the water dish, and the cookie bowl.

After Lee left, the boys and I all piled on the bed to watch the Seahawks play-off game. It felt good to have three dogs on the bed with me again. It felt especially good to have this particular dog curled up next to me. As I fell asleep that first night, with Fritz plastered against my side as Joey had always been, I smiled and knew that my relationship with this little dog would be very special.

The next morning, when I woke I looked at Fritz and told him that I didn't think his name suited him very well and asked him if he'd mind if I changed it. He didn't seem to care one way or another so I told him that I was going to call him Teddy. He just seemed more like a Teddy than a Fritz to me. Done deal.

My morning ritual with the dogs involves a walk on the beach. We do this every day, and I try not to have anything interfere with this special time we have together. So, on our first day together, Teddy hopped in the truck with the other two boys and we all went to the beach.

When we arrived at the beach, I just opened the door and all three dogs jumped out of the truck. Somehow I knew that I wouldn't ever need a leash with Teddy unless we were somewhere that required one. My feeling proved accurate because even though Teddy ran and played with the other dogs and greeted every dog and person he met like a long lost friend, he never moved very far from my side. Eventually I started calling him my "Velcro Buddy" because he was always close enough for me to touch him. Always.

As time passed, Teddy became increasingly more attentive. When I worked out in the garden he was right there with me. He was the best gardening buddy I've ever had. Not that he pulled weeds or anything. But, he was a terrific supervisor even though most of his supervising was done from a prone position with an occasional yawn thrown in just to let me know he was awake. When I was working on the computer in the study he was right there with Harper and Angus cheering me on as I conjured up words to give life to whatever I was working on at the time.

Our days were filled with gardening, reading, writing, beach walks, Old Dog Haven business, and whatever else came up on any particular day.

It was a quiet life—as mine typically is—and Teddy added his own brand of strength and consistency to the life we shared. The more time I spent with him, the more I understood why he was with me. He took pleasure in everything. Sometimes I'd see him sitting on the floor in front of the bedroom window looking out at the birds in the garden. Because he seemed to be enjoying himself so much I usually stopped what I was doing and sat down and looked out the window with him.

Among other things, Teddy taught me to look and to pay attention to what I was seeing. He lived in the moment, as all dogs do, and he taught me to do that too. Because I was still going through a grieving process my tendency was to often dwell on the past, but during those times Teddy would gently but firmly draw my attention to what was going on at that moment. He allowed me memories, but he had no tolerance for regrets. By example, he continually reminded me that life is now and joy can be found when you least expect it. His mantra seemed always to be: Pay attention. Be in the moment. Live for now.

One morning "now" became an emergency because I woke up feeling that something wasn't right with Teddy. I'm usually pretty good at reading dogs, but sometimes my own dogs tend to stonewall me, so I didn't pick up on what was going on until it was almost too late. All I got from Teddy was that his stomach hurt, so I called the vet and said I was bringing him in immediately. When I arrived and put Teddy up on the examining table my vet felt Teddy's stomach and said that there was a very large mass that needed to be removed "right now." Fortunately, both of my vets were there and they rescheduled regular appointments to perform surgery. I never leave my dogs alone at the vet so I stayed and watched while a large bloody mass the size of a football was removed. How that mass had appeared so soon was a mystery because Teddy hadn't been with me that long, and I'd had him checked when he first arrived. It wasn't there then. I also wondered why I hadn't felt it because I'm a very hands-on person when it comes to my dogs. My vet explained that growths attached to the spleen, as this one was, grow very quickly, which didn't necessarily make me feel any better, but it was an explanation I accepted. Two hours later, after both spleen and growth had been removed, I took Teddy home. He actually walked from the truck into the house, something I could hardly believe since I'd seen the surgery and the size of the incision. Very tough dog.

Long story short, Teddy made a full recovery. Ken, my vet, told me later that he didn't expect Teddy to even survive the surgery much less recover and live a healthy life for many more months. Yet another example of the resiliency and stamina of this wonderful little dog.

After Teddy recovered completely and we were back to our regular routine the lessons learned from Teddy just came rolling in every day. All of them more or less revolved around the "pay attention" concept. I've learned many things from the dogs that have shared my life, but Teddy had a way of awakening the student in me and getting my attention. He forced me, by his gentle insistence, to focus on healing and being productive. I was working on my first book when Teddy arrived, and many days the writing was a bit like wading in alphabet molasses. Harper and Angus tried to cheer me on, but they were more passive in their approach than Teddy was. Teddy just flat out insisted that I write. If I was working outside and he thought I'd been out there being distracted by gardening long enough, he'd stand in front of me until he had my attention and then he'd very deliberately walk into the house. On those occasions I knew he wasn't just going in for a nap. I knew he wanted me to follow him. More often than not he'd lead me into the study and stand in front of the computer until I sat down. I could hear him saying, "C'mon. You have thoughts in your head about those dogs. Use your words. Tell their stories." So I did.

Teddy was able to stay with me for almost two years before his body failed him. *Lymphosarcoma*—aka cancer of the lymph nodes—is often treatable, but in Teddy's case the disease manifested itself in such a way that I was only able to keep it at bay with medication for a few months before it was time to release him from his body.

Predictably, Teddy powered through bad days, constantly reassuring me that he would stay as long as I needed him. Although Teddy's attitude was admirable to say the least, I had to put aside my

Teddy and Angus

own need and do what was best for him. Finally, one morning he just crashed. I knew it was time to let him go. For me, watching a dog struggle to be well is much more difficult than the grieving that follows the death of the body, so I got out of my own way and sent my friend on to his next expression of spirit.

I've loved every dog that has shared his or her life with me—and many dogs that haven't lived with me—but Teddy was special. Not only did I love him, I needed his presence in my life exactly when he joined my little family. He was my touchstone.

Bodie, Harper, Cassie, Allen, Otis and Lacey

A PERSONAL REFLECTION

Writing this book has been a very important personal experience for me on many levels.

- It's taken about four years to gather information, photographs and do the actual writing. During this time I've had many conversations and exchanged countless emails with the people who love(d)and care(d)for the dogs featured in this book. I value those connections and the people and dogs who have made them possible.

- I feel very fortunate to be a part of the Old Dog Haven family. This wonderful organization and the people who do this labor of love are truly a family dedicated to helping old dogs and committed to the effort involved in the rescue and rehabilitation of homeless senior dogs.

- I love writing about dogs, and this book has given me an opportunity to do that and to reinforce how much dogs have to teach us.

- There hasn't been a day go by during the past four years, and even now, that I don't think about one or more of the dogs I've written about. Even though I've never actually met many of them, in telling their stories I've gotten to know all of them and feel close to them.

- This book, as with everything I write that has to do with dogs, is my way of paying it forward. What I've learned from dogs—even those I've only met through the eyes of others—has had a profound effect on the way I view life. It's all about joy and living in the moment.

- It's my hope that reading this book will inspire you to help homeless senior dogs in some way. Visit your local shelter, and if you find a senior dog in need of a home, please consider welcoming that dog into your home and heart. If you live in western Washington and would like to provide a temporary foster home for an adoptable senior dog or a permanent Final Refuge home for an old dog that isn't adoptable please contact us: office@olddoghaven.org Somewhere out there is an old dog that needs you!

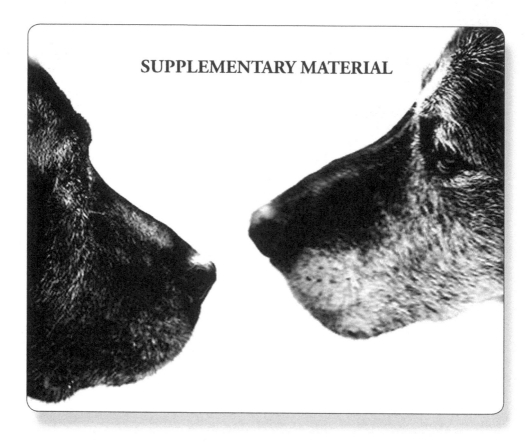

SUPPLEMENTARY MATERIAL

In the following pages you'll find three articles I wrote for the Old Dog Haven website that might be of interest and help you in some way. All the articles deal with tough issues:

- What happens to your dog if you're unable to care for him?
- Is it time to release your animal friend from his body?
- How do you deal with the grieving process after your animal companion is no longer physically with you?

Please note that I'll be using the generic "him" to refer to individual dogs rather than the awkward "him/her" reference.

Roger

PLAN AHEAD

What will happen to your dog if you are no longer able to care for him?

Many of the dogs featured in this book ended up at shelters because their people didn't make arrangements for their care in the event that they were unable to care for the dogs. Keep in mind, too, that the dogs you read about in the preceding chapters represent only a small portion of dogs that were loved by someone who died, moved to a care facility, divorced, or could no longer afford to care for a dog. This is a bigger issue than just a few dogs finding themselves homeless. **Between 40 and 50%** of the 3,400+ senior dogs Old Dog Haven has helped fall into this category, and that percentage represents only the dogs we were asked to rescue. Thousands more are ending their lives in shelters.

Don't just presume that your family or friends will assume responsibility for your senior animal friend if you are no longer able to care for him. If you don't make plans **NOW** (never mind how old you are or how secure your home situation seems) your precious friend could end up being passed from one home to another, confused and lost, only to end up in a shelter where he will die alone and afraid.

Here's what I suggest you do:

- Think carefully about the needs of your companion animal and make a decision now about who will care for him.
- Talk to family members and friends about whether they might be ready and willing to care for your dog in case you're unable to do so.
- Be sure that the person you've chosen is serious about taking on the responsibility of caring for your friend and is willing to make a commitment to you.
- Talk to the person you've chosen about your animal's needs, and make sure that this person knows the name of the dog's veterinarian. It's important that the dog's health records can be easily located.
- Give the name and phone number of the caretaker to your veterinarian and to your family if this person is not a family member.
- Include information about the caretaker in your will.
- Determine whether you'll need to provide in your will for the costs of caring for your friend.
- Keep notes about the dog's habits, needs, likes, dislikes, etc. and tell the caretaker where these notes can be found in your home.
- Keep a card in your wallet with the name, phone number and address of your caretaker so he or she can be notified immediately if you are unable to make contact.
- Finally, if you can't find anyone that you're absolutely sure will want and be able to take your senior dog into his or her home, the kindest option might be for you to consider specifying euthanasia for your dog rather than letting your friend go to a shelter.

Don't allow your dog to end up in a shelter, especially if your friend is a canine senior citizen. **Plan Ahead!**

Sparky

END-OF-LIFE DECISIONS

*How do you know when it's time to release your
animal friends from their bodies?*

Some of our old dogs leave their bodies without assistance from us. Their deaths are "natural" and require no intervention. However, one of the most difficult, yet very necessary, aspects of our work here at Old Dog Haven is making the decision to allow dogs to move on to their next expressions of spirit when their bodies fail them and their quality of life becomes seriously compromised. These dogs depend on us to help them make their transition, and we perform that final service for them with love and respect.

Every day, I talk with people who are worried about the health of their senior dog and agonizing over the end-of-life decisions that might need to be made with regard to their animal friend. If you ever find yourself in that position, perhaps the following thoughts might be of some help:

- **Quality of life is the key issue.** If your animal friend is unable to function in a way that assures you he is still enjoying a good quality of life, then it's time to seriously consider releasing him from his body. Severe incontinence caused by kidney failure, inability to eat, impaired mobility, lack of interest in surroundings, restless movement during sleep (often caused by pain), disorientation and confusion, severe vomiting, uncontrollable diarrhea, failed vision and hearing loss are all symptoms which indicate that your friend's body is failing. If you haven't already done so, make an appointment with your veterinarian to determine the seriousness of the symptoms. Ask for a blood analysis, have X-rays taken if necessary, and in short, have your veterinarian perform whatever diagnostic tests might be helpful. If there is no treatment available to radically alter the symptoms you are seeing, then it's time to release your friend. Within this context, be very careful about having painful treatments or heroic surgery performed on an old dog that is suffering. He doesn't deserve to endure more pain just because you don't want him to die. Because dogs want to be well, they often power through the pain, expending a tremendous amount of energy because they know you don't want to let them go. We don't ever want our animal friends to die, but that wanting is unreasonably self-indulgent, and allowing them to waste away and suffer isn't fulfilling your promise to care for them in all phases of their lives.

- **Don't ignore mental and emotional issues.** I talked about the devastating effects of dementia on dogs earlier in the book, and I want to be sure you take the problems that don't appear to be physical into consideration when you're thinking about what's best for your animal friend. If your dog is stressed, confused, fearful, the light is gone from his eyes, and he's no longer a joyful spirit, it's time to think about releasing him from his body.

- **Don't procrastinate** just because the decision you face is a difficult one. Have the strength to do the right thing because you love and respect your animal friend. Indulging in thoughts like "Maybe he'll be better tomorrow" only prolongs the inevitable, and will surely invite you to revisit those thoughts with strong feelings of guilt at a later date because you waited too long. Trust your intuition and rely on your connection with your animal companion. Put aside your own unwillingness to let your friend go because you will miss him. This time in your animal friend's life is not about you. It's about showing him that you love him enough to release him from his failing body.

- **Talk to your dog** about your concerns. You've established a pattern of communication with your dog that works for both of you. Let your friend know that you think it may be time to let him go. Trust that he will hear you and understand that you're ready to release him. Dogs are very loyal and intuitive companions, and if your friend understands that you're ready, he will rest easier knowing that peace will soon come to him. Don't doubt for even one minute that your friend will hear you. Dogs know what we're thinking and feeling—often far better than we do—and your thoughts and feelings will be heard.

- If you are able to draw on your reserve of strength to make the decision necessary to release your friend from his body, reach inside of yourself one more time and **stay with your dog** after you bring him to the veterinarian to have the injection that will send your friend on his way. (Some veterinarians will come to your home if you prefer to have your friend leave in a familiar setting. If you are able to arrange this, that's the best possible way of saying good-bye.) Regardless of location, your presence is very important at this most difficult time. Being able to hold your dog and feel all of the pain and discomfort slip away is a necessary conclusion to your physical friendship. Ask the veterinarian to sedate your friend so there is absolutely no discomfort involved for either of you.

- **Understand that death is just change.** Certainly you will grieve for the loss of your animal friend's physical presence, but know that you will always carry the love you shared. That permanence of spirit never changes.

Matthew

WHEN AN ANIMAL FRIEND DIES

Thoughts for those who are grieving for their companion animal

Our society allows us to grieve openly when a human friend or family member dies, but when an animal friend leaves his body sometimes the grieving rules change. If we aren't able to grieve in a way that is helpful, we're left feeling very alone in our sadness and sense of loss. Even though every situation is different, and we all have to deal with our own sorrow, these thoughts may help you put your grieving energy to positive use:

- Bury the body (or scatter the ashes) in a special place in your yard, and plant flowers or a tree to mark the spot. If you do this, you'll have a living memorial to your animal friend. After all, it's your companion's life with you that you want to remember and celebrate, not the end of the physical experience.
- If you find that you have no one to talk with about your friend, sit down and write your loving companion a letter. Allow the words that don't come easily in conversation to find their way to paper. Write down everything you feel. Tell your friend how much he meant to you. Thoughts and feelings have a way of finding their way Home regardless of how they're expressed. Trust me; your friend will hear you.

- If you have pictures of your companion, put together a photo montage. Every picture will conjure up a memory you don't want to lose. This activity can be very therapeutic and reinforce the knowledge that you shared a wonderful life together.
- Take walks in the places you and your companion favored. This is a particularly good healing experience if your friend was ill and not able to walk very well toward the end. If you really focus, you'll see him bouncing alongside of you or racing ahead in perfect health. Allow yourself to feel your friend's presence, and know that his spirit is with you.
- Think about everything your friend has taught you. Think about the lessons of pure love, devotion, patience, friendship, intuitive understanding, acceptance, playfulness and joy that you never would have learned if you hadn't been willing to welcome an animal into your life.
- If you have any regrets or "hindsight guilties," put them to rest by understanding that animals never judge. You don't need to indulge in this senseless activity either. To think "If only I had ... I wish I hadn't ... Why didn't I ...?" only prolongs your sadness and creates frustration over what can't be changed. Regardless of the circumstances of your friend's death, know that all of your actions were accepted with understanding and without judgment. If you think your friend left too soon, cherish the quality of your relationship without being sad about a life you feel was too short. Animals live in the moment, and it's important that you believe every moment you shared with your friend is significant.
- Understand that death means nothing to an animal. It's just change. The death of your friend's body allows your companion to move on to his or her next expression of spirit. What matters is that you know you've sent your friend Home with love. That forever kind of love defies any boundaries or limitations.
- Finally, please don't say that you'll "never have another" animal in your life because dealing with the death of an animal friend is too hard. To make this kind of pronouncement does a great dishonor to your friend and never allows you to use what you've learned. There are so many animals, wherever you are as you read this, that would welcome the opportunity to love and be loved. Visit your nearby shelter and see who might be there just waiting for you. Allow another animal to touch your heart. You'll know when you're ready. And when you are, don't be surprised if you hear a familiar voice whispering "Go on, pick him. You're gonna love her. I'll bet he likes to play ball too. She needs you. Share our love with your new friend."

ABOUT THE AUTHOR

Ardeth De Vries has been involved with Old Dog Haven, the largest non-profit senior dog rescue organization in the United States, since she retired from a 45-year teaching career in 2005. Currently she serves as President of the Board of Directors, and is the editor of Old Dog Haven's online newsletters as well as the print newsletters, which are available six times a year. Ardeth also writes articles for the Old Dog Haven website and counsels people about end-of-life decisions, grieving, and the care of senior dogs.

In addition to her work with Old Dog Haven, Ardeth has served on the Advisory Board of The Grey Muzzle Organization, a nonprofit group that improves the lives of at-risk senior dogs. (www.greymuzzle.org) She also operates her own nonprofit organization, Broken Arrow Memorial Fund, which provides financial assistance for veterinary care of companion animals that live on Whidbey Island in Washington state.

Ardeth has lived with special needs senior dogs for over fifty years, and she has been a volunteer at the Whidbey Island Animals' Improvement shelter for seventeen years.

Old Dog Haven: Every Old Dog Has a Story to Tell is Ardeth's third book: *First Light: Animal Voices in Concert* (Publishing Works, 2006) is a collection of stories about what animals teach us, and *A Space Between: A Journey of the Spirit* (River Sanctuary Publishing, 2010) is a metaphysical novel.

Ardeth lives on Whidbey Island in Washington state and shares her home with four senior dogs.

The author is donating all proceeds from the sale of this book to Old Dog Haven.